WHAT THE BUDDHA TAUGHT

The Buddha in walking posture at Buddhamonthon Park in Nakhon Pathom, Thailand, constructed to commemorate the 2500th year of the Buddhist Era. (Height : 15.875 metres)

WALPOLA SRI RAHULA

Tripitakavāgīśvarāchārya

What the Buddha Taught

(Revised edition)

With a Foreword by

PAUL DEMIÉVILLE

and

*a collection of illustrative texts translated from
the original Pali*

HAW TRAI

ลิขสิทธิ์ การพิมพ์ในประเทศไทยเป็นของกองทุนบุญนิธิหอไตร

ISBN 974 – 00 – 0839 – 9

Fourth published in Thailand
by Haw Trai Foundation Bangkok,
B.E. 2542 (1999)

Wat Raja-o-Rasaram
Section Thaihouse North
Khet Chomthong
Bangkok 10150
Thailand
Tel. 8937979

Printed in Thailand, (B.E. 2542) 1999

Contents

CHAPTER I

The Buddhist Attitude of Mind

Man is supreme—One is one's refuge—Responsibility—Doubt—Freedom of Thought—Tolerance—Is Buddhism Religion or Philosophy?—Truth has no label—No blind faith or belief, but seeing and understanding—No attachment even to Truth—Parable of the raft—Imaginary speculations useless—Practical attitude—Parable of the wounded man .. ..

THE FOUR NOBLE TRUTHS

CHAPTER II

The First Noble Truth: *Dukkha*

Buddhism neither pessimistic nor optimistic, but realistic—Meaning of 'Dukkha'—Three aspects of experience—Three aspects of 'Dukkha'—What is a 'being'?—Five Aggregates—No spirit opposed to matter—Flux—Thinker and Thought—Has life a beginning? .. ..

CHAPTER III

The Second Noble Truth: *Samudaya*: 'The Arising of *Dukkha*'

—Definition—Four Nutriments—Root cause of suffering and continuity—Nature of arising and cessation—Karma and Rebirth—What is death?—What is rebirth? .. ..

CHAPTER IV

The Third Noble Truth: *Nirodha*: 'The Cessation of *Dukkha*'—

What is Nirvāṇa?—Language and Absolute Truth—Definitions of Nirvāṇa—Nirvāṇa not negative—Nirvāṇa as Absolute Truth—What is Absolute Truth?—Truth is not negative—Nirvāṇa and Saṃsāra—Nirvāṇa not a result—What is there after Nirvāṇa?—Incorrect expressions—What happens to an Arahant after death?—If no Self, who realizes Nirvāṇa?—Nirvāṇa in this life .. ..

CHAPTER V

The Fourth Noble Truth: *Magga*: 'The Path'

Middle Path or Noble Eightfold Path—Compassion and Wisdom—Ethical Conduct—Mental Discipline—Wisdom—Two sorts of Understanding—Four Functions regarding the Four Noble Truths

Foreword

"What the Buddha Taught" is one of the best selling books on Buddhism in the west. It has been translated into many languages and has been reprinted several times since first being published in 1959.

The book suits people with varying degrees of knowledge of Buddhism, it includes chapters dealing with the Four Noble Truths, Buddhist Meditation, Buddhist way of life and translations of many Suttas (The Discourses of the Buddha).

I believe firmly that "What the Buddha Taught" is an extremely valuable reference book for any one who has ever been interested or curious about Buddhism. No matter how long one has been Buddhist, he is always likely to discover something new or realize how unsatisfactory his understanding of Buddhism.

Many Westerners visiting Thailand, The land of many beautiful temples, who would also like to learn something about Buddhism, will find this book ideal for them.

I met the author during my stay at Wat Buddhapadipa in London, and received a permission from him to publish his book called "What the Buddha Taught" in Thailand and no one else is permitted to use this publication in any form or any means be produced in Thailand whilst he has been authorised me to take care of his copyright.

May the truth be seen by many.

Venerable Chaokhun
Phra Metheevorrayarn

Wat Raja-o-rasaram
Chomthong (Bangkhuntien)
Bangkok 10150 Thailand   Tel. 8937979

"No God, No Brahma, can be called
The Maker of this wheel of life:
Empty phenomena roll on,
Dependent on conditions all."

(Visuddhimagga)

"By deeds, vision and righteousness,
'By virtue, the sublimest life--
'By these are mortals purified,
'And not by lineage and wealth."

(M.iii,262)

"By oneself is evil done,
By oneself is one defiled;
By oneself is evil left undone,
By oneself is one purified;
Purity and impurity depend on oneself;
No one can purity another."

(Dhammapada)

Foreword

by Paul Demiéville

Member of the Institut de France,
Professor at the College de France
Director of Buddhist Studies at the School
of Higher Studies (Paris)

Here is an exposition of Buddhism conceived in a resolutely modern spirit by one of the most qualified and enlightened representatives of that religion. The Rev. Dr. W. Rahula received the traditional training and education of a Buddhist monk in Ceylon, and held eminent positions in one of the leading monastic institutes (Pirivena) in that island, where the Law of the Buddha flourishes from the time of Asoka and has preserved all its vitality up to this day. Thus brought up in an ancient tradition, he decided, at this time when all traditions are called in question, to face the spirit and the methods of international scientific learning. He entered the Ceylon University, obtained the B.A. Honours degree (London), and then won the degree of Doctor of Philosophy of the Ceylon University on a highly learned thesis on the History of Buddhism in Ceylon. Having worked with distinguished professors at the University of Calcutta and come in contact with adepts of Mahāyāna (the Great Vehicle), that form of Buddhism which reigns from Tibet to the Far East, he decided to go into the Tibetan and Chinese texts in order to widen his œcumenism, and he has honoured us by coming to the University of Paris (Sorbonne) to prepare a study of Asanga, the illustrious philosopher of Mahāyāna, whose principal works in the original Sanskrit are lost, and can only be read in their Tibetan and Chinese translations. It is now eight years since Dr. Rahula is among us, wearing the yellow robe, breathing the air of the Occident, searching perhaps in our old troubled mirror a universalized reflection of the religion which is his.

The book, which he has kindly asked me to present to the public of the West, is a luminous account, within reach of everybody, of the fundamental principles of the Buddhist doctrine, as they are found in the most ancient texts, which are called 'The Tradition' (*Āgama*) in Sanskrit and 'The Canonic Corpus' (*Nikāya*) in Pali. Dr. Rahula, who possesses an incomparable knowledge of these texts, refers to them constantly and almost exclusively. Their authority is recognized unanimously by all the Buddhist schools, which were and are numerous, but none of which ever deviates from these texts, except with the intention of better interpreting the spirit beyond the letter. The interpretation has indeed been varied in the course of the expansion of Buddhism through many centuries and vast regions, and the Law has taken more than one aspect. But the aspect of Buddhism here presented by Dr. Rahula—humanist, rational, Socratic in some respects, Evangelic in others, or again almost scientific—has for its support a great deal of authentic scriptural evidence which he only had to let speak for themselves.

The explanations which he adds to his quotations, always translated with scrupulous accuracy, are clear, simple, direct, and free from all pedantry. Some among them might lead to discussion, as when he wishes to rediscover in the Pali sources all the doctrines of Mahāyāna; but his familiarity with those sources permits him to throw new light on them. He addresses himself to the modern man, but he refrains from insisting on comparisons just suggested here and there, which could be made with certain currents of thought of the contemporary world: socialism, atheism, existentialism, psycho-analysis. It is for the reader to appreciate the modernity, the possibilities of adaptation of a doctrine which, in this work of genuine scholarship, is presented to him in its primal richness.

Preface

All over the world today there is growing interest in Buddhism. Numerous societies and study-groups have come into being, and scores of books have appeared on the teaching of the Buddha. It is to be regretted, however, that most of them have been written by those who are not really competent, or who bring to their task misleading assumptions derived from other religions, which must misinterpret and misrepresent their subject. A professor of comparative religion who recently wrote a book on Buddhism did not even know that Ānanda, the devoted attendant of the Buddha, was a *bhikkhu* (a monk), but thought he was a layman! The knowledge of Buddhism propagated by books like these can be left to the reader's imagination.

I have tried in this little book to address myself first of all to the educated and intelligent general reader, uninstructed in the subject, who would like to know what the Buddha actually taught. For his benefit I have aimed at giving briefly, and as directly and simply as possible, a faithful and accurate account of the actual words used by the Buddha as they are to be found in the original Pali texts of the *Tipiṭaka*, universally accepted by scholars as the earliest extant records of the teachings of the Buddha. The material used and the passages quoted here are taken directly from these originals. In a few places I have referred to some later works too.

I have borne in mind, too, the reader who has already some knowledge of what the Buddha taught and would like to go further with his studies. I have therefore provided not only the Pali equivalents of most of the key-words, but also references to the original texts in footnotes, and a select bibliography.

The difficulties of my task have been manifold: throughout I have tried to steer a course between the unfamiliar and the popular, to give the English reader of the present day something which he could understand and appreciate, without sacrificing anything of the matter and the form of the discourses of the

Buddha. Writing the book I have had the ancient texts running in my mind, so I have deliberately kept the synonyms and repetitions which were a part of the Buddha's speech as it has come down to us through oral tradition, in order that the reader should have some notion of the form used by the Teacher. I have kept as close as I could to the originals, and have tried to make my translations easy and readable.

But there is a point beyond which it is difficult to take an idea without losing in the interests of simplicity the particular meaning the Buddha was interested in developing. As the title 'What the Buddha Taught' was selected for this book, I felt that it would be wrong not to set down the words of the Buddha, even the figures he used, in preference to a rendering which might provide the easy gratification of comprehensibility at the risk of distortion of meaning.

I have discussed in this book almost everything which is commonly accepted as the essential and fundamental teaching of the Buddha. These are the doctrines of the Four Noble Truths, the Noble Eightfold Path, the Five Aggregates, Karma, Rebirth, Conditioned Genesis (*Paṭiccasamuppāda*), the doctrine of No-Soul (*Anatta*), *Satipaṭṭhāna* (the Setting-up of Mindfulness). Naturally there will be in the discussion expressions which must be unfamiliar to the Western reader. I would ask him, if he is interested, to take up on his first reading the opening chapter, and then go on to Chapters V, VII and VIII, returning to Chapters II, III, IV and VI when the general sense is clearer and more vivid. It would not be possible to write a book on the teaching of the Buddha without dealing with the subjects which *Theravāda* and *Mahāyāna* Buddhism have accepted as fundamental in his system of thought.

The term *Theravāda—Hīnayāna* or 'Small Vehicle' is no longer used in informed circles—could be translated as 'the School of the Elders' (*theras*), and *Mahāyāna* as 'Great Vehicle'. They are used of the two main forms of Buddhism known in the world today. *Theravāda*, which is regarded as the original orthodox Buddhism, is followed in Ceylon, Burma, Thailand, Cambodia, Laos, and Chittagong in East Pakistan. *Mahāyāna*, which developed relatively later, is followed in other Buddhist countries like China, Japan, Tibet, Mongolia, etc. There are certain differences, mainly with regard to some beliefs, practices and observances between these two schools, but on the most important teachings of the Buddha, such as those discussed here, *Theravāda* and *Mahāyāna* are unanimously agreed.

It only remains for me now to express my sense of gratitude to Professor E. F. C. Ludowyk, who in fact invited me to write this book, for all the help given me, the interest taken in it, the suggestions he offered, and for reading through the manuscript. To Miss Marianne Möhn too, who went through the manuscript and made valuable suggestions, I am deeply grateful. Finally I am greatly beholden to Professor Paul Demiéville, my teacher in Paris, for his kindness in writing the Foreword.

W. Rahula

Paris
July 1958

TO MANI

Sabbadānaṃ dhammadānaṃ jināti
'The gift of Truth excels all other gifts'

The Buddha

The Buddha, whose personal name was Siddhattha (Siddhārtha in Sanskrit), and family name Gotama (Skt. Gautama), lived in North India in the 6th century B.C. His father, Suddhodana, was the ruler of the kingdom of the Sākyas (in modern Nepal). His mother was queen Māyā. According to the custom of the time, he was married quite young, at the age of sixteen, to a beautiful and devoted young princess named Yasodharā. The young prince lived in his palace with every luxury at his command. But all of a sudden, confronted with the reality of life and the suffering of mankind, he decided to find the solution—the way out of this universal suffering. At the age of 29, soon after the birth of his only child, Rāhula, he left his kingdom and became an ascetic in search of this solution.

For six years the ascetic Gotama wandered about the valley of the Ganges, meeting famous religious teachers, studying and following their systems and methods, and submitting himself to rigorous ascetic practices. They did not satisfy him. So he abandoned all traditional religions and their methods and went his own way. It was thus that one evening, seated under a tree (since then known as the Bodhi- or Bo-tree, 'the Tree of Wisdom'), on the bank of the river Neranjarā at Buddha-Gaya (near Gaya in modern Bihar), at the age of 35, Gotama attained Enlightenment, after which he was known as the Buddha, 'The Enlightened One'.

After his Enlightenment, Gotama the Buddha delivered his first sermon to a group of five ascetics, his old colleagues, in the Deer Park at Isipatana (modern Sarnath) near Benares. From that day, for 45 years, he taught all classes of men and women—kings and peasants, Brahmins and outcasts, bankers and beggars, holy men and robbers—without making the slightest distinction between them. He recognized no differences of caste or social groupings, and the Way he preached was open to all men and women who were ready to understand and to follow it.

At the age of 80, the Buddha passed away at Kusinārā (in modern Uttar Pradesh in India).

Today Buddhism is found in Ceylon, Burma, Thailand, Cambodia, Laos, Vietnam, Tibet, China, Japan, Mongolia, Korea, Formosa, in some parts of India, Pakistan and Nepal, and also in the Soviet Union. The Buddhist population of the world is over 500 million.

CHAPTER I

THE BUDDHIST ATTITUDE OF MIND

Among the founders of religions the Buddha (if we are permitted to call him the founder of a religion in the popular sense of the term) was the only teacher who did not claim to be other than a human being, pure and simple. Other teachers were either God, or his incarnations in different forms, or inspired by him. The Buddha was not only a human being; he claimed no inspiration from any god or external power either. He attributed all his realization, attainments and achievements to human endeavour and human intelligence. A man and only a man can become a Buddha. Every man has within himself the potentiality of becoming a Buddha, if he so wills it and endeavours. We can call the Buddha a man *par excellence*. He was so perfect in his 'human-ness' that he came to be regarded later in popular religion almost as 'super-human'.

Man's position, according to Buddhism, is supreme. Man is his own master, and there is no higher being or power that sits in judgment over his destiny.

'One is one's own refuge, who else could be the refuge?'[1] said the Buddha. He admonished his disciples to 'be a refuge to themselves', and never to seek refuge in or help from anybody else.[2] He taught, encouraged and stimulated each person to develop himself and to work out his own emancipation, for man has the power to liberate himself from all bondage through his own personal effort and intelligence. The Buddha says: 'You should do your work, for the Tathāgatas[3] only teach the way.'[4] If the Buddha is to be called a 'saviour' at all, it is only in the sense that he

---

[1]Dhp. XII 4.
[2]D II (Colombo, 1929), p. 62 (*Mahāparinibbāna-sutta*).
[3]*Tathāgata* lit. means 'One who has come to Truth', i.e., 'One who has discovered Truth'. This is the term usually used by the Buddha referring to himself and to the Buddhas in general.
[4]Dhp. XX 4.

discovered and showed the Path to Liberation, Nirvāṇa. But we must tread the Path ourselves.

It is on this principle of individual responsibility that the Buddha allows freedom to his disciples. In the *Mahāparinibbāna-sutta* the Buddha says that he never thought of controlling the *Sangha* (Order of Monks)[1], nor did he want the *Sangha* to depend on him. He said that there was no esoteric doctrine in his teaching, nothing hidden in the 'closed-fist of the teacher' (*ācariya-muṭṭhi*), or to put it in other words, there never was anything 'up his sleeve'.[2]

The freedom of thought allowed by the Buddha is unheard of elsewhere in the history of religions. This freedom is necessary because, according to the Buddha, man's emancipation depends on his own realization of Truth, and not on the benevolent grace of a god or any external power as a reward for his obedient good behaviour.

The Buddha once visited a small town called Kesaputta in the kingdom of Kosala. The inhabitants of this town were known by the common name Kālāma. When they heard that the Buddha was in their town, the Kālāmas paid him a visit, and told him:

'Sir, there are some recluses and brāhmaṇas who visit Kesaputta. They explain and illumine only their own doctrines, and despise, condemn and spurn others' doctrines. Then come other recluses and brāhmaṇas, and they, too, in their turn, explain and illumine only their own doctrines, and despise, condemn and spurn others' doctrines. But, for us, Sir, we have always doubt and perplexity as to who among these venerable recluses and brāhmaṇas spoke the truth, and who spoke falsehood.'

Then the Buddha gave them this advice, unique in the history of religions:

'Yes, Kālāmas, it is proper that you have doubt, that you have perplexity, for a doubt has arisen in a matter which is doubtful. Now, look you Kālāmas, do not be led by reports, or tradition, or hearsay. Be not led by the authority of religious texts, nor by mere logic or inference, nor by considering appearances, nor by the delight in speculative opinions, nor by seeming possibilities,

[1] *Sangha* lit. means 'Community'. But in Buddhism this term denotes 'The Community of Buddhist monks' which is the Order of Monks. Buddha, *Dhamma* (Teaching) and *Sangha* (Order) are known as *Tisaraṇa* 'Three Refuges' or *Tiratana* (Sanskrit *Triratna*) 'Triple-Gem'.

[2] D II (Colombo, 1929), p. 62.

2

nor by the idea: 'this is our teacher'. But, O Kālāmas, when you know for yourselves that certain things are unwholesome (*akusala*), and wrong, and bad, then give them up . . . And when you know for yourselves that certain things are wholesome (*kusala*) and good, then accept them and follow them.'[1]

The Buddha went even further. He told the bhikkhus that a disciple should examine even the Tathāgata (Buddha) himself, so that he (the disciple) might be fully convinced of the true value of the teacher whom he followed.[2]

According to the Buddha's teaching, doubt (*vicikicchā*) is one of the five Hindrances (*nīvaraṇa*)[3] to the clear understanding of Truth and to spiritual progress (or for that matter to any progress). Doubt, however, is not a 'sin', because there are no articles of faith in Buddhism. In fact there is no 'sin' in Buddhism, as sin is understood in some religions. The root of all evil is ignorance (*avijjā*) and false views (*micchā diṭṭhi*). It is an undeniable fact that as long as there is doubt, perplexity, wavering, no progress is possible. It is also equally undeniable that there must be doubt as long as one does not understand or see clearly. But in order to progress further it is absolutely necessary to get rid of doubt. To get rid of doubt one has to see clearly.

There is no point in saying that one should not doubt or one should believe. Just to say 'I believe' does not mean that you understand and see. When a student works on a mathematical problem, he comes to a stage beyond which he does not know how to proceed, and where he is in doubt and perplexity. As long as he has this doubt, he cannot proceed. If he wants to proceed, he must resolve this doubt. And there are ways of resolving that doubt. Just to say 'I believe', or 'I do not doubt' will certainly not solve the problem. To force oneself to believe and to accept a thing without understanding is political, and not spiritual or intellectual.

The Buddha was always eager to dispel doubt. Even just a few minutes before his death, he requested his disciples several times to ask him if they had any doubts about his teaching, and not to

---

[1] A (Colombo, 1929), p. 115.

[2] *Vimaṃsaka-sutta*, no. 47 of M.

[3] The Five Hindrances are: (1) Sensuous Lust, (2) Ill-will, (3) Physical and mental torpor and languor, (4) Restlessness and Worry, (5) Doubt.

feel sorry later that they could not clear those doubts. But the disciples were silent. What he said then was touching: 'If it is through respect for the Teacher that you do not ask anything, let even one of you inform his friend' (i.e., let one tell his friend so that the latter may ask the question on the other's behalf).[1]

Not only the freedom of thought, but also the tolerance allowed by the Buddha is astonishing to the student of the history of religions. Once in Nālandā a prominent and wealthy householder named Upāli, a well-known lay disciple of Nigaṇṭha Nātaputta (Jaina Mahāvīra), was expressly sent by Mahāvīra himself to meet the Buddha and defeat him in argument on certain points in the theory of Karma, because the Buddha's views on the subject were different from those of Mahāvīra.[2] Quite contrary to expectations, Upāli, at the end of the discussion, was convinced that the views of the Buddha were right and those of his master were wrong. So he begged the Buddha to accept him as one of his lay disciples (Upāsaka). But the Buddha asked him to reconsider it, and not to be in a hurry, for 'considering carefully is good for well-known men like you'. When Upāli expressed his desire again, the Buddha requested him to continue to respect and support his old religious teachers as he used to.[3]

In the third century B.C., the great Buddhist Emperor Asoka of India, following this noble example of tolerance and under-standing, honoured and supported all other religions in his vast empire. In one of his Edicts carved on rock, the original of which one may read even today, the Emperor declared:

'One should not honour only one's own religion and condemn the religions of others, but one should honour others' religions for this or that reason. So doing, one helps one's own religion to grow and renders service to the religions of others too. In acting otherwise one digs the grave of one's own religion and also does harm to other religions. Whosoever honours his own religion and condemns other religions, does so indeed through devotion to his own religion, thinking "I will glorify my own religion". But on the contrary, in so doing he injures his own religion more gravely.

[1]D II (Colombo, 1929), p. 95; A (Colombo, 1929), p. 239.
[2]Mahāvīra, founder of Jainism, was a contemporary of the Buddha, and was probably a few years older than the Buddha.
[3]Upāli-sutta, no. 56 of M.

4

So concord is good: Let all listen, and be willing to listen to the doctrines professed by others'.[1]

We should add here that this spirit of sympathetic understanding should be applied today not only in the matter of religious doctrine, but elsewhere as well.

This spirit of tolerance and understanding has been from the beginning one of the most cherished ideals of Buddhist culture and civilization. That is why there is not a single example of persecution or the shedding of a drop of blood in converting people to Buddhism, or in its propagation during its long history of 2500 years. It spread peacefully all over the continent of Asia, having more than 500 million adherents today. Violence in any form, under any pretext whatsoever, is absolutely against the teaching of the Buddha.

The question has often been asked: Is Buddhism a religion or a philosophy? It does not matter what you call it. Buddhism remains what it is whatever label you may put on it. The label is immaterial. Even the label 'Buddhism' which we give to the teaching of the Buddha is of little importance. The name one gives it is inessential.

What's in a name? That which we call a rose,
By any other name would smell as sweet.

In the same way Truth needs no label: it is neither Buddhist, Christian, Hindu nor Moslem. It is not the monopoly of anybody. Sectarian labels are a hindrance to the independent understanding of Truth, and they produce harmful prejudices in men's minds.

This is true not only in intellectual and spiritual matters, but also in human relations. When, for instance, we meet a man, we do not look on him as a human being, but we put a label on him, such as English, French, German, American, or Jew, and regard him with all the prejudices associated with that label in our mind. Yet he may be completely free from those attributes which we have put on him.

People are so fond of discriminative labels that they even go to the length of putting them on human qualities and emotions common to all. So they talk of different 'brands' of charity, as for example, of Buddhist charity or Christian charity, and look down

[1]Rock Edict, XII.

5

upon other 'brands' of charity. But charity cannot be sectarian; it is neither Christian, Buddhist, Hindu nor Moslem. The love of a mother for her child is neither Buddhist nor Christian: it is mother love. Human qualities and emotions like love, charity, compassion, tolerance, patience, friendship, desire, hatred, ill-will, ignorance, conceit, etc., need no sectarian labels; they belong to no particular religions.

To the seeker after Truth it is immaterial from where an idea comes. The source and development of an idea is a matter for the academic. In fact, in order to understand Truth, it is not necessary even to know whether the teaching comes from the Buddha, or from anyone else. What is essential is seeing the thing, understanding it. There is an important story in the *Majjhima-nikāya* (*sutta* no. 140) which illustrates this.

The Buddha once spent a night in a potter's shed. In the same shed there was a young recluse who had arrived there earlier.[1] They did not know each other. The Buddha observed the recluse, and thought to himself: 'Pleasant are the ways of this young man. It would be good if I should ask about him'. So the Buddha asked him: 'O bhikkhu,[2] in whose name have you left home? Or who is your master? Or whose doctrine do you like?'

'O friend,' answered the young man, 'there is the recluse Gotama, a Sakyan scion, who left the Sakya-family to become a recluse. There is high repute abroad of him that he is an Arahant, a Fully-Enlightened One. In the name of that Blessed One I have become a recluse. He is my Master, and I like his doctrine'.

'Where does that Blessed One, the Arahant, the Fully-Enlightened One live at the present time?'

'In the countries to the north, friend, there is a city called

---

[1]In India potters' sheds are spacious, and quiet. References are made in the Pali texts to ascetics and recluses, as well as to the Buddha himself, spending a night in a potter's shed during their wanderings.

[2]It is interesting to note here that the Buddha addresses this recluse as *Bhikkhu*, which term is used for Buddhist monks. In the sequel it will be seen that he was not a bhikkhu, not a member of the Order of the Sangha, for he asked the Buddha to admit him into the Order. Perhaps in the days of the Buddha the term 'bhikkhu' was used at times even for other ascetics indiscriminately, or the Buddha was not very strict in the use of the term. Bhikkhu means 'mendicant' 'one who begs food', and perhaps it was used here in its literal and original sense. But today the term 'bhikkhu' is used only of Buddhist monks, especially in Theravāda countries like Ceylon, Burma, Thailand, Cambodia, and in Chittagong.

Sāvatthi. It is there that that Blessed One, the Arahant, the Fully-Enlightened One, is now living.'

'Have you ever seen him, that Blessed One? Would you recognize him if you saw him?'

'I have never seen that Blessed One. Nor should I recognize him if I saw him.'

The Buddha realized that it was in his name that this unknown young man had left home and become a recluse. But without divulging his own identity, he said: 'O bhikkhu, I will teach you the doctrine. Listen and pay attention. I will speak.'

'Very well, friend,' said the young man in assent.

Then the Buddha delivered to this young man a most remarkable discourse explaining Truth (the gist of which is given later).[1]

It was only at the end of the discourse that this young recluse, whose name was Pukkusāti, realized that the person who spoke to him was the Buddha himself. So he got up, went before the Buddha, bowed down at the feet of the Master, and apologized to him for calling him 'friend'[2] unknowingly. He then begged the Buddha to ordain him and admit him into the Order of the Sangha.

The Buddha asked him whether he had the alms-bowl and the robes ready. (A bhikkhu must have three robes and the alms-bowl for begging food.) When Pukkusāti replied in the negative, the Buddha said that the Tathāgatas would not ordain a person unless the alms-bowl and the robes were ready. So Pukkusāti went out in search of an alms-bowl and robes, but was unfortunately savaged by a cow and died.[3]

Later, when this sad news reached the Buddha, he announced that Pukkusāti was a wise man, who had already seen Truth, and

---

[1] In the chapter on the third Noble Truth, see p. 38.

[2] The term used is *Āvuso* which means friend. It is a respectful term of address among equals. But disciples never used this term addressing the Buddha. Instead they use the term *Bhante* which approximately means 'Sir' or 'Lord'. At the time of the Buddha, the members of his Order of Monks (Sangha) addressed one another as *Āvuso* 'Friend'. But before his death the Buddha instructed younger monks to address their elders as *Bhante* 'Sir' or *Āyasmā* 'Venerable'. But elders should address the younger members by name, or as *Āvuso* 'Friend'. (D II Colombo, 1929, p. 95). This practice is continued up to the present day in the Sangha.

[3] It is well-known that cows in India roam about the streets. From this reference it seems that the tradition is very old. But generally these cows are docile and not savage or dangerous.

7

attained the penultimate stage in the realization of Nirvāṇa, and that he was born in a realm where he would become an Arahant[1] and finally pass away, never to return to this world again[2].

From this story it is quite clear that when Pukkusāti listened to the Buddha and understood his teaching, he did not know who was speaking to him, or whose teaching it was. He saw Truth. If the medicine is good, the disease will be cured. It is not necessary to know who prepared it, or where it came from.

Almost all religions are built on faith—rather 'blind' faith it would seem. But in Buddhism emphasis is laid on 'seeing', knowing, understanding, and not on faith, or belief. In Buddhist texts there is a word *saddhā* (Skt. *śraddhā*) which is usually translated as 'faith' or 'belief'. But *saddhā* is not 'faith' as such, but rather 'confidence' born out of conviction. In popular Buddhism and also in ordinary usage in the texts the word *saddhā*, it must be admitted, has an element of 'faith' in the sense that it signifies devotion to the Buddha, the *Dhamma* (Teaching) and the *Sangha* (The Order).

According to Asanga, the great Buddhist philosopher of the 4th century A.C., *śraddhā* has three aspects: (1) full and firm conviction that a thing is, (2) serene joy at good qualities, and (3) aspiration or wish to achieve an object in view.[3]

However you put it, faith or belief as understood by most religions has little to do with Buddhism.[4]

The question of belief arises when there is no seeing—seeing in every sense of the word. The moment you see, the question of belief disappears. If I tell you that I have a gem hidden in the folded palm of my hand, the question of belief arises because you

---

[1] An *Arahant* is a person who has liberated himself from all defilements and impurities such as desire, hatred, ill-will, ignorance, pride, conceit, etc. He has attained the fourth or the highest and ultimate stage in the realization of Nirvāṇa, and is full of wisdom, compassion and such pure and noble qualities. Pukkusāti had attained at the moment only the third stage which is technically called *Anāgāmi* 'Never-Returner'. The second stage is called *Sakadāgāmi* 'Once-Returner' and the first stage is called *Sotāpanna* 'Stream-Entrant'.

[2] Karl Gjellerup's *The Pilgrim Kamanita* seems to have been inspired by this story of Pukkusāti.

[3] Abhisamuc, p. 6.

[4] *The Role of the Miracle in Early Pali Literature* by Edith Ludowyk-Gyomroi takes up this subject. Unfortunately this Ph.D. thesis is not yet published. On the same subject see an article by the same author in the University of Ceylon Review, Vol. 1, No. 1 (April, 1943), p. 74 ff.

do not see it yourself. But if I unclench my fist and show you the gem, then you see it for yourself, and the question of belief does not arise. So the phrase in ancient Buddhist texts reads: 'Realizing, as one sees a gem (or a myrobalan fruit) in the palm'.

A disciple of the Buddha named Musīla tells another monk: 'Friend Savittha, without devotion, faith or belief,[1] without liking or inclination, without hearsay or tradition, without considering apparent reasons, without delight in the speculations of opinions, I know and see that the cessation of becoming is Nirvāṇa.'[2]

And the Buddha says: 'O bhikkhus, I say that the destruction of defilement and impurities is (meant) for a person who knows and who sees, and not for a person who does not know and does not see.'[3]

It is always a question of knowing and seeing, and not that of believing. The teaching of the Buddha is qualified as *ehi-passika*, inviting you to 'come and see', but not to come and believe.

The expressions used everywhere in Buddhist texts referring to persons who realized Truth are: 'The dustless and stainless Eye of Truth (*Dhamma-cakkhu*) has arisen.' 'He has seen Truth, has attained Truth, has known Truth, has penetrated into Truth, has crossed over doubt, is without wavering.' 'Thus with right wisdom he sees it as it is (*yathā bhūtaṃ*)'.[4] With reference to his own Enlightenment the Buddha said: 'The eye was born, knowledge was born, wisdom was born, science was born, light was born.'[5] It is always seeing through knowledge or wisdom (*ñāṇa-dassana*), and not believing through faith.

This was more and more appreciated at a time when Brāhmaṇic orthodoxy intolerantly insisted on believing and accepting their tradition and authority as the only Truth without question. Once a group of learned and well-known Brahmins went to see the Buddha and had a long discussion with him. One of the group, a Brahmin youth of 16 years of age, named Kāpaṭhika, considered

---

[1]Here the word *saddhā* is used in its ordinary popular sense of 'devotion, faith, belief'.
[2]S II (PTS.), p. 117.
[3]*Ibid.* III, p. 152.
[4]E.g. S V, (PTS), p. 423; III, p. 103; M III (PTS), p. 19.
[5]S V (PTS), p. 422.

by them all to be an exceptionally brilliant mind, put a question to the Buddha:[1]

'Venerable Gotama, there are the ancient holy scriptures of the Brahmins handed down along the line by unbroken oral tradition of texts. With regard to them, Brahmins come to the absolute conclusion: "This alone is Truth, and everything else is false". Now, what does the Venerable Gotama say about this?'

The Buddha inquired: 'Among Brahmins is there any one single Brahmin who claims that he personally knows and sees that "This alone is Truth, and everything else is false."?'

The young man was frank, and said: 'No'.

'Then, is there any one single teacher, or a teacher of teachers of Brahmins back to the seventh generation, or even any one of those original authors of those scriptures, who claims that he knows and he sees: "This alone is Truth, and everything else is false"?'

'No.'

'Then, it is like a line of blind men, each holding on to the preceding one; the first one does not see, the middle one also does not see, the last one also does not see. Thus, it seems to me that the state of the Brahmins is like that of a line of blind men.'

Then the Buddha gave advice of extreme importance to the group of Brahmins: 'It is not proper for a wise man who maintains (lit. protects) truth to come to the conclusion: "This alone is Truth, and everything else is false".'

Asked by the young Brahmin to explain the idea of maintaining or protecting truth, the Buddha said: 'A man has a faith. If he says "This is my faith", so far he maintains truth. But by that he cannot proceed to the absolute conclusion: "This alone is Truth, and everything else is false".' In other words, a man may believe what he likes, and he may say 'I believe this'. So far he respects truth. But because of his belief or faith, he should not say that what he believes is alone the Truth, and everything else is false.

The Buddha says: 'To be attached to one thing (to a certain view) and to look down upon other things (views) as inferior—this the wise men call a fetter.'[2]

[1]*Cankī-sutta*, no. 95 of M.
[2]Sn (PTS), p. 151 (v. 798).

Once the Buddha explained[1] the doctrine of cause and effect to his disciples, and they said that they saw it and understood it clearly. Then the Buddha said:

'O bhikkhus, even this view, which is so pure and so clear, if you cling to it, if you fondle it, if you treasure it, if you are attached to it, then you do not understand that the teaching is similar to a raft, which is for crossing over, and not for getting hold of.'[2]

Elsewhere the Buddha explains this famous simile in which his teaching is compared to a raft for crossing over, and not for getting hold of and carrying on one's back:

'O bhikkhus, a man is on a journey. He comes to a vast stretch of water. On this side the shore is dangerous, but on the other it is safe and without danger. No boat goes to the other shore which is safe and without danger, nor is there any bridge for crossing over. He says to himself: "This sea of water is vast, and the shore on this side is full of danger; but on the other shore it is safe and without danger. No boat goes to the other side, nor is there a bridge for crossing over. It would be good therefore if I would gather grass, wood, branches and leaves to make a raft, and with the help of the raft cross over safely to the other side, exerting myself with my hands and feet". Then that man, O bhikkhus, gathers grass, wood, branches and leaves and makes a raft, and with the help of that raft crosses over safely to the other side, exerting himself with his hands and feet. Having crossed over and got to the other side, he thinks: "This raft was of great help to me. With its aid I have crossed safely over to this side, exerting myself with my hands and feet. It would be good if I carry this raft on my head or on my back wherever I go".

'What do you think, O bhikkhus, if he acted in this way would that man be acting properly with regard to the raft? "No, Sir". In which way then would he be acting properly with regard to the raft? Having crossed and gone over to the other side, suppose that man should think: "This raft was a great help to me. With its aid I have crossed safely over to this side, exerting myself with my hands and feet. It would be good if I beached this raft on the shore, or moored it and left it afloat, and then went on my way

[1] In the *Mahātaṇhāsaṅkhaya-sutta*, no. 38 of M.
[2] M I (PTS), p. 260.

wherever it may be". Acting in this way would that man act properly with regard to that raft.

'In the same manner, O bhikkhus, I have taught a doctrine similar to a raft—it is for crossing over, and not for carrying (lit. getting hold of). You, O bhikkhus, who understand that the teaching is similar to a raft, should give up even good things (*dhamma*); how much more then should you give up evil things (*adhamma*).'[1]

From this parable it is quite clear that the Buddha's teaching is meant to carry man to safety, peace, happiness, tranquillity, the attainment of *Nirvāṇa*. The whole doctrine taught by the Buddha leads to this end. He did not say things just to satisfy intellectual curiosity. He was a practical teacher and taught only those things which would bring peace and happiness to man.

The Buddha was once staying in a Siṃsapā forest in Kosambi (near Allahabad). He took a few leaves into his hand, and asked his disciples: 'What do you think, O bhikkhus? Which is more? These few leaves in my hand or the leaves in the forest over here?'

'Sir, very few are the leaves in the hand of the Blessed One, but indeed the leaves in the Siṃsapā forest over here are very much more abundant.'

'Even so, bhikkhus, of what I have known I have told you only a little, what I have not told you is very much more. And why have I not told you (those things)? Because that is not useful . . . not leading to *Nirvāṇa*. That is why I have not told you those things.'[2]

It is futile, as some scholars vainly try to do, for us to speculate on what the Buddha knew but did not tell us.

The Buddha was not interested in discussing unnecessary metaphysical questions which are purely speculative and which create imaginary problems. He considered them as a 'wilderness of opinions'. It seems that there were some among his own disciples who did not appreciate this attitude of his. For, we have

[1]M I (PTS), pp. 134-135. *Dhamma* here, according to the Commentary, means high spiritual attainments as well as pure views and ideas. Attachment even to these, however high and pure they may be, should be given up; how much more then should it be with regard to evil and bad things. MA II (PTS), p. 109.

[2]S V (PTS), p. 437.

the example of one of them, Māluṅkyaputta by name, who put to the Buddha ten well-known classical questions on metaphysical problems and demanded answers.[1]

One day Māluṅkyaputta got up from his afternoon meditation, went to the Buddha, saluted him, sat on one side and said:

'Sir, when I was all alone meditating, this thought occurred to me: There are these problems unexplained, put aside and rejected by the Blessed One. Namely, (1) is the universe eternal or (2) is it not eternal, (3) is the universe finite or (4) is it infinite, (5) is soul the same as body or (6) is soul one thing and body another thing, (7) does the Tathāgata exist after death, or (8) does he not exist after death, or (9) does he both (at the same time) exist and not exist after death, or (10) does he both (at the same time) not exist and not not-exist. These problems the Blessed One does not explain to me. This (attitude) does not please me, I do not appreciate it. I will go to the Blessed One and ask him about this matter. If the Blessed One explains them to me, then I will continue to follow the holy life under him. If he does not explain them, I will leave the Order and go away. If the Blessed One knows that the universe is eternal, let him explain it to me so. If the Blessed One knows that the universe is not eternal, let him say so. If the Blessed One does not know whether the universe is eternal or not, etc., then for a person who does not know, it is straightforward to say "I do not know, I do not see".'

The Buddha's reply to Māluṅkyaputta should do good to many millions in the world today who are wasting valuable time on such metaphysical questions and unnecessarily disturbing their peace of mind:

'Did I ever tell you, Māluṅkyaputta, "Come, Māluṅkyaputta, lead the holy life under me, I will explain these questions to you?"'

'No, Sir.'

'Then, Māluṅkyaputta, even you, did you tell me: "Sir, I will lead the holy life under the Blessed One, and the Blessed One will explain these questions to me"?'

'No, Sir.'

'Even now, Māluṅkyaputta, I do not tell you: "Come and lead the holy life under me, I will explain these questions to you".

---

[1] *Cūla-Māluṅkya-sutta*, no. 63 of M.

13

And you do not tell me either: "Sir, I will lead the holy life under the Blessed One, and he will explain these questions to me". Under these circumstances, you foolish one, who refuses whom?[1]

'Māluṅkyaputta, if anyone says: "I will not lead the holy life under the Blessed One until he explains these questions," he may die with these questions unanswered by the Tathāgata. Suppose Māluṅkyaputta, a man is wounded by a poisoned arrow, and his friends and relatives bring him to a surgeon. Suppose the man should then say: "I will not let this arrow be taken out until I know who shot me; whether he is a Kṣatriya (of the warrior caste) or a Brāhmaṇa (of the priestly caste) or a Vaiśya (of the trading and agricultural caste) or a Sūdra (of the low caste); what his name and family may be; whether he is tall, short, or of medium stature; whether his complexion is black, brown, or golden; from which village, town or city he comes. I will not let this arrow be taken out until I know the kind of bow with which I was shot; the kind of bowstring used; the type of arrow; what sort of feather was used on the arrow and with what kind of material the point of the arrow was made." Māluṅkyaputta, that man would die without knowing any of these things. Even so, Māluṅkyaputta, if anyone says: "I will not follow the holy life under the Blessed One until he answers these questions such as whether the universe is eternal or not, etc.," he would die with these questions unanswered by the Tathāgata.'

Then the Buddha explains to Māluṅkyaputta that the holy life does not depend on these views. Whatever opinion one may have about these problems, there is birth, old age, decay, death, sorrow, lamentation, pain, grief, distress, "the Cessation of which (i.e. Nirvāṇa) I declare in this very life."

'Therefore, Māluṅkyaputta, bear in mind what I have explained as explained, and what I have not explained as unexplained. What are the things that I have not explained? Whether the universe is eternal or not, etc., (those 10 opinions) I have not explained. Why, Māluṅkyaputta, have I not explained them? Because it is not useful, it is not fundamentally connected with the spiritual holy life, is not conducive to aversion, detachment, cessation, tranquillity, deep penetration, full realization, Nirvāṇa. That is why I have not told you about them.

[1] i.e., both are free and neither is under obligation to the other.

'Then, what, Māluṅkyaputta, have I explained? I have explained *dukkha*, the arising of *dukkha*, the cessation of *dukkha*, and the way leading to the cessation of *dukkha*.[1] Why, Māluṅkyaputta, have I explained them? Because it is useful, is fundamentally connected with the spiritual holy life, is conducive to aversion, detachment, cessation, tranquillity, deep penetration, full realization, Nirvāṇa. Therefore I have explained them.'[2]

Let us now examine the Four Noble Truths which the Buddha told Māluṅkyaputta he had explained.

[1]These Four Noble Truths are explained in the next four chapters.

[2]It seems that this advice of the Buddha had the desired effect on Māluṅkyaputta, because elsewhere he is reported to have approached the Buddha again for instruction, following which he became an Arahant. A (Colombo, 1929), pp. 345-346; S IV (PTS), p. 72 ff.

CHAPTER II

The Four Noble Truths

THE FIRST NOBLE TRUTH: *DUKKHA*

The heart of the Buddha's teaching lies in the Four Noble Truths (*Cattāri Ariyasaccāni*) which he expounded in his very first sermon[1] to his old colleagues, the five ascetics, at Isipatana (modern Sarnath) near Benares. In this sermon, as we have it in the original texts, these four Truths are given briefly. But there are innumerable places in the early Buddhist scriptures where they are explained again and again, with greater detail and in different ways. If we study the Four Noble Truths with the help of these references and explanations, we get a fairly good and accurate account of the essential teachings of the Buddha according to the original texts.

The Four Noble Truths are:

1. *Dukkha*[2]
2. *Samudaya*, the arising or origin of *dukkha*,
3. *Nirodha*, the cessation of *dukkha*,
4. *Magga*, the way leading to the cessation of *dukkha*.

THE FIRST NOBLE TRUTH: *DUKKHA*

The First Noble Truth (*Dukkha-ariyasacca*) is generally translated by almost all scholars as 'The Noble Truth of Suffering', and it is interpreted to mean that life according to Buddhism is nothing but suffering and pain. Both translation and interpretation are highly unsatisfactory and misleading. It is because of this limited, free and easy translation, and its superficial interpretation, that many people have been misled into regarding Buddhism as pessimistic.

---

[1] *Dhammacakkappavattana-sutta* 'Setting in Motion the Wheel of Truth'. Mhvg. (Alutgama, 1922), p. 9 ff; S V (PTS). p. 420 ff.

[2] I do not wish to give an equivalent in English for this term for reasons given below.

Phra Buddhajinaraj of Wat Phra Sriratana Mahatat is said to be one of the most beautiful Buddha images in Thailand. (17th century B.E. or 12th century A.D.)

Colossal stone statues at Gal-vihāra,
Polnnaruva, Sri Lanka

First of all, Buddhism is neither pessimistic nor optimistic. If anything at all, it is realistic, for it takes a realistic view of life and of the world. It looks at things objectively (*yathābhūtaṃ*). It does not falsely lull you into living in a fool's paradise, nor does it frighten and agonize you with all kinds of imaginary fears and sins. It tells you exactly and objectively what you are and what the world around you is, and shows you the way to perfect freedom, peace, tranquillity and happiness.

One physician may gravely exaggerate an illness and give up hope altogether. Another may ignorantly declare that there is no illness and that no treatment is necessary, thus deceiving the patient with a false consolation. You may call the first one pessimistic and the second optimistic. Both are equally dangerous. But a third physician diagnoses the symptoms correctly, understands the cause and the nature of the illness, sees clearly that it can be cured, and courageously administers a course of treatment, thus saving his patient. The Buddha is like the last physician. He is the wise and scientific doctor for the ills of the world (*Bhisakka* or *Bhaiṣajya-guru*).

It is true that the Pali word *dukkha* (or Sanskrit *duḥkha*) in ordinary usage means 'suffering', 'pain', 'sorrow' or 'misery', as opposed to the word *sukha* meaning 'happiness', 'comfort' or 'ease'. But the term *dukkha* as the First Noble Truth, which represents the Buddha's view of life and the world, has a deeper philosophical meaning and connotes enormously wider senses. It is admitted that the term *dukkha* in the First Noble Truth contains, quite obviously, the ordinary meaning of 'suffering', but in addition it also includes deeper ideas such as 'imperfection', 'impermanence', 'emptiness', 'insubstantiality'. It is difficult therefore to find one word to embrace the whole conception of the term *dukkha* as the First Noble Truth, and so it is better to leave it untranslated, than to give an inadequate and wrong idea of it by conveniently translating it as 'suffering' or 'pain'.

The Buddha does not deny happiness in life when he says there is suffering. On the contrary he admits different forms of happiness, both material and spiritual, for laymen as well as for monks. In the *Aṅguttara-nikāya*, one of the five original Collections in Pāli containing the Buddha's discourses, there is a list of happinesses (*sukhāni*), such as the happiness of family life and the happiness of the life of a recluse, the happiness of sense pleasures and the happiness of renunciation, the happiness of attachment and the happiness of detachment, physical happiness and mental happiness etc.[1] But all these are included in *dukkha*. Even the very pure spiritual states of *dhyāna* (*recueillement* or trance) attained by the practice of higher meditation, free from even a shadow of suffering in the accepted sense of the word, states which may be described as unmixed happiness, as well as the state of *dhyāna* which is free from sensations both pleasant (*sukha*) and unpleasant (*dukkha*) and is only pure equanimity and awareness—even these very high spiritual states are included in *dukkha*. In one of the *suttas* of the *Majjhima-nikāya*, (again one of the five original Collections), after praising the spiritual happiness of these *dhyānas*, the Buddha says that they are 'impermanent, *dukkha*, and subject to change' (*aniccā dukkhā vipariṇāmadhammā*).[2] Notice that the word *dukkha* is explicitly used. It is *dukkha*, not because there is 'suffering' in the ordinary sense of the word, but because 'whatever is impermanent is *dukkha*' (*yad aniccaṃ taṃ dukkhaṃ*).

The Buddha was realistic and objective. He says, with regard to life and the enjoyment of sense-pleasures, that one should clearly understand three things: (1) attraction or enjoyment (*assāda*), (2) evil consequence or danger or unsatisfactoriness (*ādīnava*), and (3) freedom or liberation (*nissaraṇa*).[3] When you see a pleasant, charming and beautiful person, you like him (or her), you are attracted, you enjoy seeing that person again and again, you derive pleasure and satisfaction from that person. This is enjoyment (*assāda*). It is a fact of experience. But this enjoyment is not permanent, just as that person and all his (or her) attractions are not permanent either. When the situation changes, when you cannot see that person, when you are deprived of this enjoyment, you become sad, you may become unreasonable and unbalanced, you may even behave foolishly. This is the evil, unsatisfactory and dangerous side of the picture (*ādīnava*). This, too, is a fact of experience. Now if you have no attachment to the person, if you are completely detached, that is freedom, liberation

[1] A (Colombo, 1929), p. 49.
[2] *Mahādukkhakkhandha-sutta*, M I (PTS), p. 90.
[3] M I (PTS), p. 85 ff; S III (PTS), p. 27 ff.

18

(*nissaraṇa*). These three things are true with regard to all enjoyment in life.

From this it is evident that it is no question of pessimism or optimism, but that we must take account of the pleasures of life as well as of its pains and sorrows, and also of freedom from them, in order to understand life completely and objectively. Only then is true liberation possible. Regarding this question the Buddha says:

'O bhikkhus, if any recluses or brāhmaṇas do not understand objectively in this way that the enjoyment of sense-pleasures is enjoyment, that their unsatisfactoriness is unsatisfactoriness, that liberation from them is liberation, then it is not possible that they themselves will certainly understand the desire for sense-pleasures completely, or that they will be able to instruct another person to that end, or that the person following their instruction will completely understand the desire for sense-pleasures. But, O bhikkhus, if any recluses or brāhmaṇas understand objectively in this way that the enjoyment of sense-pleasures is enjoyment, that their unsatisfactoriness is unsatisfactoriness, that liberation from them is liberation, then it is possible that they themselves will certainly understand the desire for sense-pleasures completely, and that they will be able to instruct another person to that end, and that that person following their instruction will completely understand the desire for sense-pleasures.'[1]

The conception of *dukkha* may be viewed from three aspects: (1) *dukkha* as ordinary suffering (*dukkha-dukkha*), (2) *dukkha* as produced by change (*vipariṇāma-dukkha*) and (3) *dukkha* as conditioned states (*saṃkhāra-dukkha*).[2]

All kinds of suffering in life like birth, old age, sickness, death, association with unpleasant persons and conditions, separation from beloved ones and pleasant conditions, not getting what one desires, grief, lamentation, distress—all such forms of physical and mental suffering, which are universally accepted as suffering or pain, are included in *dukkha* as ordinary suffering (*dukkha-dukkha*).

[1]M I (PTS), p. 87.
[2]Vism (PTS), p. 499; Abhisamuc, p. 38.

A happy feeling, a happy condition in life, is not permanent, not everlasting. It changes sooner or later. When it changes, it produces pain, suffering, unhappiness. This vicissitude is included in *dukkha* as suffering produced by change (*vipariṇāma-dukkha*).

It is easy to understand the two forms of suffering (*dukkha*) mentioned above. No one will dispute them. This aspect of the First Noble Truth is more popularly known because it is easy to understand. It is common experience in our daily life.

But the third form of *dukkha* as conditioned states (*saṃkhāra-dukkha*) is the most important philosophical aspect of the First Noble Truth, and it requires some analytical explanation of what we consider as a 'being', as an 'individual', or as 'I'.

What we call a 'being', or an 'individual', or 'I', according to Buddhist philosophy, is only a combination of ever-changing physical and mental forces or energies, which may be divided into five groups or aggregates (*pañcakkhandha*). The Buddha says: 'In short these five aggregates of attachment are *dukkha*'.[1] Elsewhere he distinctly defines *dukkha* as the five aggregates: 'O bhikkhus, what is *dukkha*? It should be said that it is the five aggregates of attachment'.[2] Here it should be clearly understood that *dukkha* and the five aggregates are not two different things; the five aggregates themselves are *dukkha*. We will understand this point better when we have some notion of the five aggregates which constitute the so-called 'being'. Now, what are these five?

The Five Aggregates

The first is the Aggregate of Matter (*Rūpakkhandha*). In this term 'Aggregate of Matter' are included the traditional Four Great Elements (*cattāri mahābhūtāni*), namely, solidity, fluidity, heat and motion, and also the Derivatives (*upādāya-rūpa*) of the Four Great Elements.[3] In the term 'Derivatives of Four Great Elements' are included our five material sense-organs, i.e., the faculties of eye, ear, nose, tongue, and body, and their corresponding objects in the external world, i.e., visible form, sound, odour, taste,

---

[1] *Saṃkhittena pañcupādānakkhandhā dukkhā.* S V (PTS), p. 421.
[2] S III (PTS), p. 158.
[3] S III (PTS), p. 59.

and tangible things, and also some thoughts or ideas or conceptions which are in the sphere of mind-objects (*dharmāyatana*)[1]. Thus the whole realm of matter, both internal and external, is included in the Aggregate of Matter.

The second is the Aggregate of Sensations (*Vedanākkhandha*). In this group are included all our sensations, pleasant or unpleasant or neutral, experienced through the contact of physical and mental organs with the external world. They are of six kinds: the sensations experienced through the contact of the eye with visible forms, ear with sounds, nose with odour, tongue with taste, body with tangible objects, and mind (which is the sixth faculty in Buddhist Philosophy) with mind-objects or thoughts or ideas.[2] All our physical and mental sensations are included in this group.

A word about what is meant by the term 'Mind' (*manas*) in Buddhist philosophy may be useful here. It should clearly be understood that mind is not spirit as opposed to matter. It should always be remembered that Buddhism does not recognize a spirit opposed to matter, as is accepted by most other systems of philosophies and religions. Mind is only a faculty or organ (*indriya*) like the eye or the ear. It can be controlled and developed like any other faculty, and the Buddha speaks quite often of the value of controlling and disciplining these six faculties. The difference between the eye and the mind as faculties is that the former senses the world of colours and visible forms, while the latter senses the world of ideas and thoughts and mental objects. We experience different fields of the world with different senses. We cannot hear colours, but we can see them. Nor can we see sounds, but we can hear them. Thus with our five physical sense-organs—eye, ear, nose, tongue, body—we experience only the world of visible forms, sounds, odours, tastes and tangible objects. But these represent only a part of the world, not the whole world. What of ideas and thoughts? They are also a part of the world. But they cannot be sensed, they cannot be conceived by the faculty of the eye, ear, nose, tongue or body. Yet they can be conceived by another faculty, which is mind. Now ideas and

[1]Abhisamuc, p. 4. Vibh. p. 72. Dhs. p. 133 § 594.
[2]S III (PTS), p. 59.

thoughts are not independent of the world experienced by these five physical sense faculties. In fact they depend on, and are conditioned by, physical experiences. Hence a person born blind cannot have ideas of colour, except through the analogy of sounds or some other things experienced through his other faculties. Ideas and thoughts which form a part of the world are thus produced and conditioned by physical experiences and are conceived by the mind. Hence mind (*manas*) is considered a sense faculty or organ (*indriya*), like the eye or the ear.

The third is the Aggregate of Perceptions (*Saññākkhandha*). Like sensations, perceptions also are of six kinds, in relation to six internal faculties and the corresponding six external objects. Like sensations, they are produced through the contact of our six faculties with the external world. It is the perceptions that recognize objects whether physical or mental.[1]

The fourth is the Aggregate of Mental Formations[2] (*Saṃkhārakkhandha*). In this group are included all volitional activities both good and bad. What is generally known as *karma* (or *kamma*) comes under this group. The Buddha's own definition of *karma* should be remembered here: 'O bhikkhus, it is volition (*cetanā*) that I call *karma*. Having willed, one acts through body, speech and mind.'[3] Volition is 'mental construction, mental activity. Its function is to direct the mind in the sphere of good, bad or neutral activities.'[4] Just like sensations and perceptions, volition is of six kinds, connected with the six internal faculties and the corresponding six objects (both physical and mental) in the external world.[5] Sensations and perceptions are not volitional actions. They do not produce karmic effects. It is only volitional actions— such as attention (*manasikāra*), will (*chanda*), determination (*adhimokkha*), confidence (*saddhā*), concentration (*samādhi*), wisdom (*paññā*), energy (*viriya*), desire (*rāga*), repugnance or hate (*paṭigha*)

---

[1]S III (PTS), p. 60.

[2]'Mental Formations' is a term now generally used to represent the wide meaning of the word *saṃkhāra* in the list of Five Aggregates. *Saṃkhāra* in other contexts may mean anything conditioned, anything in the world, in which sense all the Five Aggregates are *saṃkhāra*.

[3]A (Colombo, 1929), p. 590—*Cetanā'haṃ bhikkhave kammaṃ vadāmi. Cetayitvā kammaṃ karoti kāyena vācā manasā.*

[4]Abhisamuc, p. 6.

[5]S III (PTS), p. 60.

ignorance (*avijjā*), conceit (*māna*), idea of self (*sakkāya-diṭṭhi*) etc. —that can produce karmic effects. There are 52 such mental activities which constitute the Aggregate of Mental Formations. The fifth is the Aggregate of Consciousness (*Viññāṇakkhandha*).[1] Consciousness is a reaction or response which has one of the six faculties (eye, ear, nose, tongue, body and mind) as its basis, and one of the six corresponding external phenomena (visible form, sound, odour, taste, tangible things and mind-objects, i.e., an idea or thought) as its object. For instance, visual consciousness (*cakkhu-viññāṇa*) has the eye as its basis and a visible form as its object. Mental consciousness (*mano-viññāṇa*) has the mind (*manas*) as its basis and a mental object, i.e., an idea or thought (*dhamma*) as its object. So consciousness is connected with other faculties. Thus, like sensation, perception and volition, consciousness also is of six kinds, in relation to six internal faculties and corresponding six external objects.[2]

It should be clearly understood that consciousness does not recognize an object. It is only a sort of awareness—awareness of the presence of an object. When the eye comes in contact with a colour, for instance blue, visual consciousness arises which simply is awareness of the presence of a colour; but it does not recognize that it is blue. There is no recognition at this stage. It is perception (the third Aggregate discussed above) that recognizes that it is blue. The term 'visual consciousness' is a philosophical expression denoting the same idea as is conveyed by the ordinary word 'seeing'. Seeing does not mean recognizing. So are the other forms of consciousness.

It must be repeated here that according to Buddhist philosophy there is no permanent, unchanging spirit which can be considered 'Self', or 'Soul', or 'Ego', as opposed to matter, and that consciousness (*viññāṇa*) should not be taken as 'spirit' in opposition to matter. This point has to be particularly emphasized, because a wrong notion that consciousness is a sort of Self or Soul that

[1]According to Mahāyāna Buddhist philosophy the Aggregate of Consciousness has three aspects: *citta, manas* and *vijñāna*, and the *Ālaya-vijñāna* (popularly translated as 'Store-Consciousness') finds its place in this Aggregate. A detailed and comparative study of this subject will be found in a forthcoming work on Buddhist philosophy by the present writer.

[2]S III (PTS), p. 61.

23

continues as a permanent substance through life, has persisted from the earliest time to the present day.

One of the Buddha's own disciples, Sāti by name, held that the Master taught: 'It is the same consciousness that transmigrates and wanders about.' The Buddha asked him what he meant by 'consciousness'. Sāti's reply is classical: 'It is that which expresses, which feels, which experiences the results of good and bad deeds here and there'.

'To whomever, you stupid one', remonstrated the Master, 'have you heard me expounding the doctrine in this manner? Haven't I in many ways explained consciousness as arising out of conditions: that there is no arising of consciousness without conditions.' Then the Buddha went on to explain consciousness in detail: 'Conciousness is named according to whatever condition through which it arises: on account of the eye and visible forms arises a consciousness, and it is called visual consciousness; on account of the ear and sounds arises a consciousness, and it is called auditory consciousness; on account of the nose and odours arises a consciousness, and it is called olfactory consciousness; on account of the tongue and tastes arises a consciousness, and it is called gustatory consciousness; on account of the body and tangible objects arises a consciousness, and it is called tactile consciousness; on account of the mind and mind-objects (ideas and thoughts) arises a consciousness, and it is called mental consciousness.'

Then the Buddha explained it further by an illustration: A fire is named according to the material on account of which it burns. A fire may burn on account of wood, and it is called wood-fire. It may burn on account of straw, and then it is called straw-fire. So consciousness is named according to the condition through which it arises.[1]

Dwelling on this point, Buddhaghosa, the great commentator, explains: '. . . a fire that burns on account of wood burns only when there is a supply, but dies down in that very place when it (the supply) is no longer there, because then the condition has changed, but (the fire) does not cross over to splinters, etc., and

[1] *Mahātaṇhāsaṃkhaya-sutta*, M I (PTS), p. 256 ff.

24

become a splinter-fire and so on; even so the consciousness that arises on account of the eye and visible forms arises in that gate of sense organ (i.e., in the eye), only when there is the condition of the eye, visible forms, light and attention, but ceases then and there when it (the condition) is no more there, because then the condition has changed, but (the consciousness) does not cross over to the ear, etc., and become auditory consciousness and so on . . .'[1]

The Buddha declared in unequivocal terms that consciousness depends on matter, sensation, perception and mental formations, and that it cannot exist independently of them. He says:

'Consciousness may exist having matter as its means (*rūpupāyaṃ*), matter as its object (*rūpārammaṇaṃ*), matter as its support (*rūpapatiṭṭhaṃ*), and seeking delight it may grow, increase and develop; or consciousness may exist having sensation as its means . . . or perception as its means . . . or mental formations as its means, mental formations as its object, mental formations as its support, and seeking delight it may grow, increase and develop.

'Were a man to say: I shall show the coming, the going, the passing away, the arising, the growth, the increase or the development of consciousness apart from matter, sensation, perception and mental formations, he would be speaking of something that does not exist.'[2]

Very briefly these are the five Aggregates. What we call a 'being', or an 'individual', or 'I', is only a convenient name or a label given to the combination of these five groups. They are all impermanent, all constantly changing. 'Whatever is impermanent is *dukkha*' (*Yad aniccaṃ taṃ dukkhaṃ*). This is the true meaning of the Buddha's words: 'In brief the five Aggregates of Attachment are *dukkha*.' They are not the same for two consecutive moments. Here A is not equal to A. They are in a flux of momentary arising and disappearing.

'O Brāhmaṇa, it is just like a mountain river, flowing far and swift, taking everything along with it; there is no moment, no instant, no second when it stops flowing, but it goes on flowing and

---

[1]MA II (PTS), pp. 306-307.
[2]S III (PTS), p. 58.

continuing. So Brāhmaṇa, is human life, like a mountain river.'[1] As the Buddha told Raṭṭhapāla: 'The world is in continuous flux and is impermanent.'

One thing disappears, conditioning the appearance of the next in a series of cause and effect. There is no unchanging substance in them. There is nothing behind them that can be called a permanent Self (*Ātman*), individuality, or anything that can in reality be called 'I'. Every one will agree that neither matter, nor sensation, nor perception, nor any one of those mental activities, nor consciousness can really be called 'I'.[2] But when these five physical and mental aggregates which are interdependent are working together in combination as a physio-psychological machine,[3] we get the idea of 'I'. But this is only a false idea, a mental formation, which is nothing but one of those 52 mental formations of the fourth Aggregate which we have just discussed, namely, it is the idea of self (*sakkāya-diṭṭhi*).

These five Aggregates together, which we popularly call a 'being', are *dukkha* itself (*saṃkhāra-dukkha*). There is no other 'being' or 'I', standing behind these five aggregates, who experiences *dukkha*. As Buddhaghosa says:

'Mere suffering exists, but no sufferer is found;
The deeds are, but no doer is found.'[4]

There is no unmoving mover behind the movement. It is only movement. It is not correct to say that life is moving, but life is movement itself. Life and movement are not two different things. In other words, there is no thinker behind the thought. Thought itself is the thinker. If you remove the thought, there is no thinker to be found. Here we cannot fail to notice how this Buddhist view is diametrically opposed to the Cartesian *cogito ergo sum*: 'I think, therefore I am.'

Now a question may be raised whether life has a beginning.

[1]A (Colombo, 1929), p. 700. These words are attributed by the Buddha to a Teacher (*Satthā*) named Araka who was free from desires and who lived in the dim past. It is interesting to remember here the doctrine of Heraclitus (about 500 B.C.) that everything is in a state of flux, and his famous statement: 'You cannot step twice into the same river, for fresh waters are ever flowing in upon you.'

[2]The doctrine of Anatta 'No-Self' will be discussed in Chapter VI.

[3]In fact Buddhaghosa compares a 'being' to a wooden mechanism (*dāruyanta*). Vism. (PTS), pp. 594-595.

[4]Vism. (PTS), p. 513.

According to the Buddha's teaching the beginning of the life-stream of living beings is unthinkable. The believer in the creation of life by God may be astonished at this reply. But if you were to ask him 'What is the beginning of God?' he would answer without hesitation 'God has no beginning', and he is not astonished at his own reply. The Buddha says: 'O bhikkhus, this cycle of continuity (*saṃsāra*) is without a visible end, and the first beginning of beings wandering and running round, enveloped in ignorance (*avijjā*) and bound down by the fetters of thirst (desire, *taṇhā*) is not to be perceived.'[1] And further, referring to ignorance which is the main cause of the continuity of life the Buddha states: 'The first beginning of ignorance (*avijjā*) is not to be perceived in such a way as to postulate that there was no ignorance beyond a certain point.'[2] Thus it is not possible to say that there was no life beyond a certain definite point.

This in short is the meaning of the Noble Truth of *Dukkha*. It is extremely important to understand this First Noble Truth clearly because, as the Buddha says, 'he who sees *dukkha* sees also the arising of *dukkha*, sees also the cessation of *dukkha*, and sees also the path leading to the cessation of *dukkha*.'[3]

This does not at all make the life of a Buddhist melancholy or sorrowful, as some people wrongly imagine. On the contrary, a true Buddhist is the happiest of beings. He has no fears or anxieties. He is always calm and serene, and cannot be upset or dismayed by changes or calamities, because he sees things as they are. The Buddha was never melancholy or gloomy. He was described by his contemporaries as 'ever-smiling' (*mihita-pubbaṃgama*). In Buddhist painting and sculpture the Buddha is always represented with a countenance happy, serene, contented and compassionate. Never a trace of suffering or agony or pain is to be seen.[4] Buddhist art and architecture, Buddhist temples

[1]S II (PTS), pp. 178-179; III pp. 149, 151.
[2]A V (PTS), p. 113.
[3]S V (PTS), p. 437. In fact the Buddha says that he who sees any one of the Four Noble Truths sees the other three as well. These Four Noble Truths are interconnected.
[4]There is a statue from Gandhara, and also one from Fou-Kien, China, depicting Gotama as an ascetic, emaciated, with all his ribs showing. But this was before his Enlightenment, when he was submitting himself to the rigorous ascetic practices which he condemned after he became Buddha.

never give the impression of gloom or sorrow, but produce an atmosphere of calm and serene joy.

Although there is suffering in life, a Buddhist should not be gloomy over it, should not be angry or impatient at it. One of the principal evils in life, according to Buddhism, is 'repugnance' or hatred. Repugnance (*pratigha*) is explained as 'ill-will with regard to living beings, with regard to suffering and with regard to things pertaining to suffering. Its function is to produce a basis for unhappy states and bad conduct.'[1] Thus it is wrong to be impatient at suffering. Being impatient or angry at suffering does not remove it. On the contrary, it adds a little more to one's troubles, and aggravates and exacerbates a situation already disagreeable. What is necessary is not anger or impatience, but the understanding of the question of suffering, how it comes about, and how to get rid of it, and then to work accordingly with patience, intelligence, determination and energy.

There are two ancient Buddhist texts called the *Theragāthā* and *Therīgāthā* which are full of the joyful utterances of the Buddha's disciples, both male and female, who found peace and happiness in life through his teaching. The king of Kosala once told the Buddha that unlike many a disciple of other religious systems who looked haggard, coarse, pale, emaciated and unprepossessing, his disciples were 'joyful and elated (*haṭṭha-pahaṭṭha*), jubilant and exultant (*udaggudagga*), enjoying the spiritual life (*abhiratarūpa*), with faculties pleased (*pīṇitindriya*), free from anxiety (*appossukka*), serene (*pannaloma*), peaceful (*paradavutta*) and living with a gazelle's mind (*migabhūtena cetasā*), i.e., light-hearted.' The king added that he believed that this healthy disposition was due to the fact that 'these venerable ones had certainly realized the great and full significance of the Blessed One's teaching.'[2]

Buddhism is quite opposed to the melancholic, sorrowful, penitent and gloomy attitude of mind which is considered a hindrance to the realization of Truth. On the other hand, it is interesting to remember here that joy (*pīti*) is one of the seven *Bojjhaṃgas* or 'Factors of Enlightenment', the essential qualities to be cultivated for the realization of Nirvāṇa.[3]

[1]Abhisamuc, p. 7.
[2]M II (PTS), p. 121.
[3]For these Seven Factors of Enlightenment see Chapter on Meditation, p. 75.

CHAPTER III

THE SECOND NOBLE TRUTH:

S A M U D A Y A : 'The Arising of *Dukkha*'

The Second Noble Truth is that of the arising or origin of *dukkha* (*Dukkhasamudaya-ariyasacca*). The most popular and well-known definition of the Second Truth as found in innumerable places in the original texts runs as follows:

'It is this "thirst" (craving, *taṇhā*) which produces re-existence and re-becoming (*ponobhavikā*), and which is bound up with passionate greed (*nandīrāgasahagatā*), and which finds fresh delight now here and now there (*tatratatrābhinandinī*), namely, (1) thirst for sense-pleasures (*kāma-taṇhā*), (2) thirst for existence and becoming (*bhava-taṇhā*) and (3) thirst for non-existence (self-annihilation, *vibhava-taṇhā*).'[1]

It is this 'thirst', desire, greed, craving, manifesting itself in various ways, that gives rise to all forms of suffering and the continuity of beings. But it should not be taken as the first cause, for there is no first cause possible as, according to Buddhism, everything is relative and inter-dependent. Even this 'thirst', *taṇhā*, which is considered as the cause or origin of *dukkha*, depends for its arising (*samudaya*) on something else, which is sensation (*vedanā*),[2] and sensation arises depending on contact (*phassa*), and so on and so forth goes on the circle which is known as Conditioned Genesis (*Paṭicca-samuppāda*), which we will discuss later.[3]

So *taṇhā*, 'thirst', is not the first or the only cause of the arising of *dukkha*. But it is the most palpable and immediate cause, the 'principal thing' and the 'all-pervading thing'.[4] Hence in certain

---

[1]Mhvg. (Alutgama, 1922), p. 9; S V (PTS), p. 421 and *passim*.
[2]*Vedanāsamudayā taṇhāsamudayo.* M I (PTS), p. 51.
[3]See p. 53.
[4]Abhisamuc, p. 43, *prādhānyārtha, sarvatragārtha.*

places of the original Pali texts themselves the definition of *samudaya* or the origin of *dukkha* includes other defilements and impurities (*kilesā, sāsavā dhammā*), in addition to *taṇhā* 'thirst' which is always given the first place.[1] Within the necessarily limited space of our discussion, it will be sufficient if we remember that this 'thirst' has as its centre the false idea of self arising out of ignorance.

Here the term 'thirst' includes not only desire for, and attachment to, sense-pleasures, wealth and power, but also desire for, and attachment to, ideas and ideals, views, opinions, theories, conceptions and beliefs (*dhamma-taṇhā*).[2] According to the Buddha's analysis, all the troubles and strife in the world, from little personal quarrels in families to great wars between nations and countries, arise out of this selfish 'thirst'.[3] From this point of view, all economic, political and social problems are rooted in this selfish 'thirst'. Great statesmen who try to settle international disputes and talk of war and peace only in economic and political terms touch the superficialities, and never go deep into the real root of the problem. As the Buddha told Raṭṭapāla: 'The world lacks and hankers, and is enslaved to "thirst" (*taṇhādāso*).'

Every one will admit that all the evils in the world are produced by selfish desire. This is not difficult to understand. But how this desire, 'thirst', can produce re-existence and re-becoming (*ponobhavikā*) is a problem not so easy to grasp. It is here that we have to discuss the deeper philosophical side of the Second Noble Truth corresponding to the philosophical side of the First Noble Truth. Here we must have some idea about the theory of *karma* and rebirth.

There are four Nutriments (*āhāra*) in the sense of 'cause' or 'condition' necessary for the existence and continuity of beings: (1) ordinary material food (*kabaliṅkārāhāra*), (2) contact of our sense-organs (including mind) with the external world (*phassāhāra*), (3) consciousness (*viññāṇāhara*) and (4) mental volition or will (*manosañcetanāhāra*).[4]

---

[1] See Vibh. (PTS), p. 106 ff.
[2] M I (PTS), p. 51; S II p. 72; Vibh. p. 380.
[3] M I, p. 86.
[4] *ibid.*, p. 48.

Of these four, the last mentioned 'mental volition' is the will to live, to exist, to re-exist, to continue, to become more and more.[1] It creates the root of existence and continuity, striving forward by way of good and bad actions (*kusalākusalakamma*).[2] It is the same as 'Volition' (*cetanā*).[3] We have seen earlier[4] that volition is karma, as the Buddha himself has defined it. Referring to 'Mental volition' just mentioned above the Buddha says: 'When one understands the nutriment of mental volition one understands the three forms of 'thirst' (*taṇhā*).'[5] Thus the terms 'thirst', 'volition', 'mental volition' and 'karma' all denote the same thing: they denote the desire, the will to be, to exist, to re-exist, to become more and more, to grow more and more, to accumulate more and more. This is the cause of the arising of *dukkha*, and this is found within the Aggregate of Mental Formations, one of the Five Aggregates which constitute a being.[6]

Here is one of the most important and essential points in the Buddha's teaching. We must therefore clearly and carefully mark and remember that the cause, the germ, of the arising of *dukkha* is within *dukkha* itself, and not outside; and we must equally well remember that the cause, the germ, of the cessation of *dukkha*, of the destruction of *dukkha*, is also within *dukkha* itself, and not outside. This is what is meant by the well-known formula often found in original Pali texts: *Yaṃ kiñci samudayadhammaṃ sabbaṃ taṃ nirodhadhammaṃ* 'Whatever is of the nature of arising, all that is of the nature of cessation.'[7] A being, a thing, or a system, if it has within itself the nature of arising, the nature of coming into being, has also within itself the nature, the germ, of its own cessation and destruction. Thus *dukkha* (Five Aggregates) has within itself the nature of its own arising, and has also within

---

[1]It is interesting to compare this 'mental volition' with 'libido' in modern psychology.

[2]MA I (PTS), p. 210.

[3]*Manosañcetanā' ti cetanā eva vuccati*. MA I (PTS), p. 209.

[4]See above p. 22.

[5]S II (PTS), p. 100. The three forms of 'thirst' are: (1) Thirst for sense-pleasures, (2) Thirst for existence and becoming, and (3) Thirst for non-existence, as given in the definition of *samudaya* 'arising of *dukkha*' above.

[6]See above p. 22.

[7]M III (PTS), p. 280; S IV, pp. 47, 107; V, p. 423 and *passim*.

itself the nature of its own cessation. This point will be taken up again in the discussion of the Third Noble Truth, *Nirodha*.

Now, the Pali word *kamma* or the Sanskrit word *karma* (from the root *kṛ* to do) literally means 'action', 'doing'. But in the Buddhist theory of karma it has a specific meaning: it means only 'volitional action', not all action. Nor does it mean the result of karma as many people wrongly and loosely use it. In Buddhist terminology karma never means its effect; its effect is known as the 'fruit' or the 'result' of karma (*kamma-phala* or *kamma-vipāka*).

Volition may relatively be good or bad, just as a desire may relatively be good or bad. So karma may be good or bad relatively. Good karma (*kusala*) produces good effects, and bad karma (*akusala*) produces bad effects. 'Thirst', volition, karma, whether good or bad, has one force as its effect: force to continue—to continue in a good or bad direction. Whether good or bad it is relative, and is within the cycle of continuity (*saṃsāra*). An Arahant, though he acts, does not accumulate karma, because he is free from the false idea of self, free from the 'thirst' for continuity and becoming, free from all other defilements and impurities (*kilesā, sāsavā dhammā*). For him there is no rebirth.

The theory of karma should not be confused with so-called 'moral justice' or 'reward and punishment'. The idea of moral justice, or reward and punishment, arises out of the conception of a supreme being, a God, who sits in judgment, who is a law-giver and who decides what is right and wrong. The term 'justice' is ambiguous and dangerous, and in its name more harm than good is done to humanity. The theory of karma is the theory of cause and effect, of action and reaction; it is a natural law, which has nothing to do with the idea of justice or reward and punishment. Every volitional action produces its effects or results. If a good action produces good effects and a bad action bad effects, it is not justice, or reward, or punishment meted out by anybody or any power sitting in judgment on your action, but this is in virtue of its own nature, its own law. This is not difficult to understand. But what is difficult is that, according to the karma theory, the effects of a volitional action may continue to manifest themselves even in a life after death. Here we have to explain what death is according to Buddhism.

We have seen earlier that a being is nothing but a combination

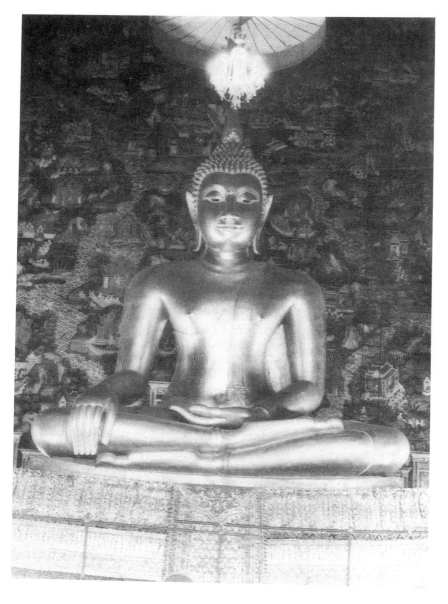

Phra Sri Sakya Muni, the great bronze Buddha of the Sukhothai period, was brought down from Sukhothai to Bangkok during the reign of King Rama I and enshrined at Wat Suthatthephavararam, Bangkok, Thailand.

Daibutsu, Great Buddha—Kamakura, Japan

The Buddha—from Mathura, India

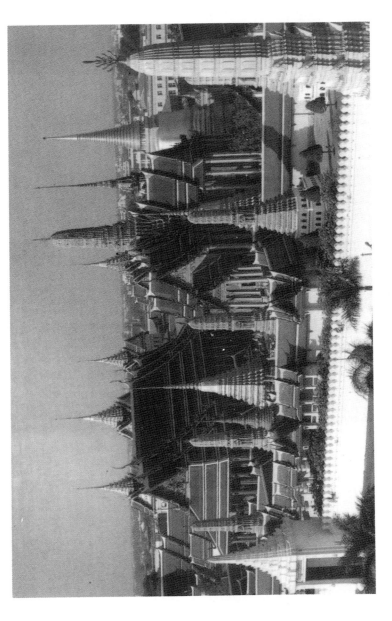

Located in the grounds of the Grand Palace is the Temple of the Emerald Buddha, Thailand's most revered Buddha image. This is the royal chapel built by King Rama I of the Chakri dynasty in 2310 B.E. (1767 A.D.)

of physical and mental forces or energies. What we call death is the total non-functioning of the physical body. Do all these forces and energies stop altogether with the non-functioning of the body? Buddhism says 'No'. Will, volition, desire, thirst to exist, to continue, to become more and more, is a tremendous force that moves whole lives, whole existences, that even moves the whole world. This is the greatest force, the greatest energy in the world. According to Buddhism, this force does not stop with the non-functioning of the body, which is death; but it continues manifesting itself in another form, producing re-existence which is called rebirth.

Now, another question arises: If there is no permanent, unchanging entity or substance like Self or Soul (*ātman*), what is it that can re-exist or be reborn after death? Before we go on to life after death, let us consider what this life is, and how it continues now. What we call life, as we have so often repeated, is the combination of the Five Aggregates, a combination of physical and mental energies. These are constantly changing; they do not remain the same for two consecutive moments. Every moment they are born and they die. 'When the Aggregates arise, decay and die, O bhikkhu, every moment you are born, decay and die.'[1] Thus, even now during this life time, every moment we are born and die, but we continue. If we can understand that in this life we can continue without a permanent, unchanging substance like Self or Soul, why can't we understand that those forces themselves can continue without a Self or a Soul behind them after the non-functioning of the body?

When this physical body is no more capable of functioning, energies do not die with it, but continue to take some other shape or form, which we call another life. In a child all the physical, mental and intellectual faculties are tender and weak, but they have within them the potentiality of producing a full grown man. Physical and mental energies which constitute the so-called being have within themselves the power to take a new form, and grow gradually and gather force to the full.

[1] Prmj. I (PTS), p. 78. '*Khandhesu jāyamānesu jīyamānesu mīyamānesu ca khaṇe khaṇe tvaṃ bhikkhu jāyase ca jīyase ca mīyase ca.*' This is quoted in the *Paramatthajotikā* Commentary as the Buddha's own words. So far I have not been able to trace this passage back to its original text.

As there is no permanent, unchanging substance, nothing passes from one moment to the next. So quite obviously, nothing permanent or unchanging can pass or transmigrate from one life to the next. It is a series that continues unbroken, but changes every moment. The series is, really speaking, nothing but movement. It is like a flame that burns through the night: it is not the same flame nor is it another. A child grows up to be a man of sixty. Certainly the man of sixty is not the same as the child of sixty years ago, nor is he another person. Similarly, a person who dies here and is reborn elsewhere is neither the same person, nor another (*na ca so na ca añño*). It is the continuity of the same series. The difference between death and birth is only a thought-moment: the last thought-moment in this life conditions the first thought-moment in the so-called next life, which, in fact, is the continuity of the same series. During this life itself, too, one thought-moment conditions the next thought-moment. So from the Buddhist point of view, the question of life after death is not a great mystery, and a Buddhist is never worried about this problem.

As long as there is this 'thirst' to be and to become, the cycle of continuity (*saṃsāra*) goes on. It can stop only when its driving force, this 'thirst', is cut off through wisdom which sees Reality, Truth, Nirvāṇa.

CHAPTER IV

THE THIRD NOBLE TRUTH:

NIRODHA : 'The Cessation of *Dukkha*'

The Third Noble Truth is that there is emancipation, liberation, freedom from suffering, from the continuity of *dukkha*. This is called the Noble Truth of the Cessation of *dukkha* (*Dukkhanirodha-ariyasacca*), which is *Nibbāna*, more popularly known in its Sanskrit form of *Nirvāṇa*.

To eliminate *dukkha* completely one has to eliminate the main root of *dukkha*, which is 'thirst' (*taṇhā*), as we saw earlier. Therefore Nirvāṇa is known also by the term *Taṇhakkhaya* 'Extinction of Thirst'.

Now you will ask: But what is Nirvāṇa? Volumes have been written in reply to this quite natural and simple question; they have, more and more, only confused the issue rather than clarified it. The only reasonable reply to give to the question is that it can never be answered completely and satisfactorily in words, because human language is too poor to express the real nature of the Absolute Truth or Ultimate Reality which is Nirvāṇa. Language is created and used by masses of human beings to express things and ideas experienced by their sense organs and their mind. A supramundane experience like that of the Absolute Truth is not of such a category. Therefore there cannot be words to express that experience, just as the fish had no words in his vocabulary to express the nature of the solid land. The tortoise told his friend the fish that he (the tortoise) just returned to the lake after a walk on the land. 'Of course' the fish said, 'You mean swimming.' The tortoise tried to explain that one couldn't swim on the land, that it was solid, and that one walked on it. But the fish insisted that there could be nothing like it, that it must be liquid like his lake, with waves, and that one must be able to dive and swim there.

35

Words are symbols representing things and ideas known to us; and these symbols do not and cannot convey the true nature of even ordinary things. Language is considered deceptive and misleading in the matter of understanding of the Truth. So the *Laṅkāvatāra-sūtra* says that ignorant people get stuck in words like an elephant in the mud.[1]

Nevertheless we cannot do without language. But if Nirvāṇa is to be expressed and explained in positive terms, we are likely immediately to grasp an idea associated with those terms, which may be quite the contrary. Therefore it is generally expressed in negative terms[2]—a less dangerous mode perhaps. So it is often referred to by such negative terms as *Taṇhakkhaya* 'Extinction of Thirst', *Asaṃkhata* 'Uncompound', 'Unconditioned', *Virāga* 'Absence of desire', *Nirodha* 'Cessation', *Nibbāna* 'Blowing out' or 'Extinction'.

Let us consider a few definitions and descriptions of Nirvāṇa as found in the original Pali texts:

'It is the complete cessation of that very 'thirst' (*taṇhā*), giving it up, renouncing it, emancipation from it, detachment from it.'[3]

'Calming of all conditioned things, giving up of all defilements, extinction of "thirst", detachment, cessation, Nibbāna.'[4]

'O bhikkhus, what is the Absolute (*Asaṃkhata*, Unconditioned)? It is, O bhikkhus, the extinction of desire (*rāgakkhayo*) the extinction of hatred (*dosakkhayo*), the extinction of illusion (*mohakkhayo*). This, O bhikkhus, is called the Absolute.'[5]

'O Rādha, the extinction of "thirst" (*Taṇhakkhayo*) is Nibbāna.'[6]

'O bhikkhus, whatever there may be things conditioned or unconditioned, among them detachment (*virāga*) is the highest.

---

[1] Lanka. p. 113.

[2] Sometimes positive terms like *Siva* 'Auspicious', 'Good', *Khema* 'Safety', *Suddhi* 'Purity', *Dīpa* 'Island', *Saraṇa* 'Refuge', *Tāṇa* 'Protection', *Pāra* 'Opposite shore', 'Other side', *Santi* 'Peace', 'Tranquillity' are used to denote Nirvāṇa. There are 32 synonyms for Nibbāna in the *Asaṃkhata-saṃyutta* of the *Saṃyutta-nikāya*. They are mostly metaphorical.

[3] Mhvg. (Alutgama, 1922), p. 10; S V p. 421. It is interesting to note that this definition of *Nirodha* 'Cessation of *Dukkha*', which is found in the first sermon of the Buddha at Sarnath, does not contain the word *Nibbāna*, though the definition means it.

[4] S I, p. 136.

[5] *Ibid.* IV, p. 359.

[6] *Ibid.* III, p. 190.

36

That is to say, freedom from conceit, destruction of thirst,[1] the uprooting of attachment, the cutting off of continuity, the extinction of "thirst" (*taṇhā*), detachment, cessation, Nibbāna.'[2]

The reply of Sāriputta, the chief disciple of the Buddha, to a direct question 'What is Nibbāna?' posed by a Parivrājaka, is identical with the definition of *Asaṃkhata* given by the Buddha (above): 'The extinction of desire, the extinction of hatred, the extinction of illusion.'[3]

'The abandoning and destruction of desire and craving for these Five Aggregates of Attachment: that is the cessation of *dukkha*.'[4]

'The cessation of Continuity and becoming (*Bhavanirodha*) is Nibbāna.'[5]

And further, referring to Nirvāṇa the Buddha says:

'O bhikkhus, there is the unborn, ungrown, and unconditioned. Were there not the unborn, ungrown, and unconditioned, there would be no escape for the born, grown, and conditioned. Since there is the unborn, ungrown, and unconditioned, so there is escape for the born, grown, and conditioned.'[6]

'Here the four elements of solidity, fluidity, heat and motion have no place; the notions of length and breadth, the subtle and the gross, good and evil, name and form are altogether destroyed; neither this world nor the other, nor coming, going or standing, neither death nor birth, nor sense-objects are to be found.'[7]

Because Nirvāṇa is thus expressed in negative terms, there are many who have got a wrong notion that it is negative, and expresses self-annihilation. Nirvāṇa is definitely no annihilation of self, because there is no self to annihilate. If at all, it is the annihilation of the illusion, of the false idea of self.

It is incorrect to say that Nirvāṇa is negative or positive. The ideas of 'negative' and 'positive' are relative, and are within the

---

[1]Here the word *pipāsa* which lit. means thirst.
[2]A (PTS) II, p. 34.
[3]S (PTS) IV, p. 251.
[4]Sāriputta's words. M I, (PTS), p. 191.
[5]Words of Musīla, another disciple of the Buddha. S II (PTS), p. 117.
[6]Ud. (Colombo, 1929), p. 129.
[7]*Ibid.* p. 128; D I (Colombo, 1929), p. 172.

realm of duality. These terms cannot be applied to Nirvāṇa, Absolute Truth, which is beyond duality and relativity.

A negative word need not necessarily indicate a negative state. The Pali of Sanskrit word for health is *ārogya*, a negative term, which literally means 'absence or illness'. But *ārogya* (health) does not represent a negative state. The word 'Immortal' (or its Sanskrit equivalent *Amṛta* or Pali *Amata*), which also is a synonym for Nirvāṇa, is negative, but it does not denote a negative state. The negation of negative values is not negative. One of the well-known synonyms for Nirvāṇa is 'Freedom' (Pali *Mutti*, Skt. *Mukti*). Nobody would say that freedom is negative. But even freedom has a negative side: freedom is always a liberation from something which is obstructive, which is evil, which is negative. But freedom is not negative. So Nirvāṇa, *Mutti* or *Vimutti*, the Absolute Freedom, is freedom from all evil, freedom from craving, hatred and ignorance, freedom from all terms of duality, relativity, time and space.

We may get some idea of Nirvāṇa as Absolute Truth from the *Dhātuvibhaṅga-sutta* (No. 140) of the *Majjhima-nikāya*. This extremely important discourse was delivered by the Buddha to Pukkusāti (already mentioned), whom the Master found to be intelligent and earnest, in the quiet of the night in a potter's shed. The essence of the relevant portions of the sutta is as follows:

A man is composed of six elements: solidity, fluidity, heat, motion, space and consciousness. He analyses them and finds that none of them is 'mine', or 'me', or 'my self'. He understands how consciousness appears and disappears, how pleasant, unpleasant and neutral sensations appear and disappear. Through this knowledge his mind becomes detached. Then he finds within him a pure equanimity (*upekhā*), which he can direct towards the attainment of any high spiritual state, and he knows that thus this pure equanimity will last for a long period. But then he thinks:

'If I focus this purified and cleansed equanimity on the Sphere of Infinite Space and develop a mind conforming thereto, that is a mental creation (*saṃkhataṃ*).[1] If I focus this purified and cleansed equanimity on the Sphere of Infinite Consciousness . . . on the

---

[1]Notice that all the spiritual and mystic states, however pure and high they may be, are mental creations, mind-made, conditioned and compound (*saṃkhata*). They are not Reality, not Truth (*sacca*).

Sphere of Nothingness . . . or on the Sphere of Neither-perception nor Non-perception and develop a mind conforming thereto, that is a mental creation.' Then he neither mentally creates nor wills continuity and becoming (*bhava*) or annihilation (*vibhava*).[1] As he does not construct or does not will continuity and becoming or annihilation, he does not cling to anything in the world; as he does not cling, he is not anxious; as he is not anxious, he is completely calmed within (fully blown out within *paccattaṃ yeva parinibbāyati*). And he knows: 'Finished is birth, lived is pure life, what should be done is done, nothing more is left to be done.'[2]

Now, when he experiences a pleasant, unpleasant or neutral sensation, he knows that it is impermanent, that it does not bind him, that it is not experienced with passion. Whatever may be the sensation, he experiences it without being bound to it (*visaṃyutto*). He knows that all those sensations will be pacified with the dissolution of the body, just as the flame of a lamp goes out when oil and wick give out.

'Therefore, O bhikkhu, a person so endowed is endowed with the absolute wisdom, for the knowledge of the extinction of all *dukkha* is the absolute noble wisdom.

'This his deliverance, founded on Truth, is unshakable. O bhikkhu, that which is unreality (*mosadhamma*) is false; that which is reality (*amosadhamma*), Nibbāna, is Truth (*Sacca*). Therefore, O bhikkhu, a person so endowed is endowed with this Absolute Truth. For, the Absolute Noble Truth (*paramaṃ ariyasaccaṃ*) is Nibbāna, which is Reality.'

Elsewhere the Buddha unequivocally uses the word Truth in place of Nibbāna: 'I will teach you the Truth and the Path leading to the Truth.'[3] Here Truth definitely means Nirvāṇa.

Now, what is Absolute Truth? According to Buddhism, the Absolute Truth is that there is nothing absolute in the world, that everything is relative, conditioned and impermanent, and that there is no unchanging, everlasting, absolute substance like Self, Soul or *Ātman* within or without. This is the Absolute

---

[1]This means that he does not produce new karma, because now he is free from 'thirst', will, volition.

[2]This expression means that now he is an Arahant.

[3]S V (PTS), p. 369.

Truth. Truth is never negative, though there is a popular expression as negative truth. The realization of this Truth, i.e., to see things as they are (*yathābhūtaṃ*) without illusion or ignorance (*avijjā*),[1] is the extinction of craving 'thirst' (*Taṇhakkhaya*), and the cessation (*Nirodha*) of *dukkha*, which is Nirvāṇa. It is interesting and useful to remember here the Mahāyāna view of Nirvāṇa as not being different from *Saṃsāra*.[2] The same thing is Saṃsāra or Nirvāṇa according to the way you look at it—subjectively or objectively. This Mahāyāna view was probably developed out of the ideas found in the original Theravāda Pali texts, to which we have just referred in our brief discussion.

It is incorrect to think that Nirvāṇa is the natural result of the extinction of craving. Nirvāṇa is not the result of anything. If it would be a result, then it would be an effect produced by a cause. It would be *saṃkhata* 'produced' and 'conditioned'. Nirvāṇa is neither cause nor effect. It is beyond cause and effect. Truth is not a result nor an effect. It is not produced like a mystic, spiritual, mental state, such as *dhyāna* or *samādhi*. TRUTH IS. NIRVĀṆA IS. The only thing you can do is to see it, to realize it. There is a path leading to the realization of Nirvāṇa. But Nirvāṇa is not the result of this path.[3] You may get to the mountain along a path, but the mountain is not the result, not an effect of the path. You may see a light, but the light is not the result of your eyesight.

People often ask: What is there after Nirvāṇa? This question cannot arise, because Nirvāṇa is the Ultimate Truth. If it is Ultimate, there can be nothing after it. If there is anything after Nirvāṇa, then that will be the Ultimate Truth and not Nirvāṇa. A monk named Rādha put this question to the Buddha in a different form: 'For what purpose (or end) is Nirvāṇa?' This question presupposes something after Nirvāṇa, when it postulates some purpose or end for it. So the Buddha answered: 'O Rādha, this question could not catch its limit (i.e., it is beside the

---

[1]Cf. *Lanka*. p. 200; 'O Mahāmati, Nirvāṇa means to see the state of things as they are.'

[2]Nāgārjuna clearly says that '*Saṃsāra* has no difference whatever from Nirvāṇa and Nirvāṇa has no difference whatever from *Saṃsāra*.' (Madhya. Kari XXV, 19).

[3]It is useful to remember here that among nine supra-mundane *dharmas* (*navalokuttara-dhamma*) Nirvāṇa is beyond *magga* (path) and *phala* (fruition).

point). One lives the holy life with Nirvāṇa as its final plunge (into the Absolute Truth), as its goal, as its ultimate end.'[1]

Some popular inaccurately phrased expressions like 'The Buddha entered into Nirvāṇa or Parinirvāṇa after his death' have given rise to many imaginary speculations about Nirvāṇa.[2] The moment you hear the phrase that 'the Buddha entered into Nirvāṇa or Parinirvāṇa', you take Nirvāṇa to be a state, or a realm, or a position in which there is some sort of existence, and try to imagine it in terms of the senses of the word 'existence' as it is known to you. This popular expression 'entered into Nirvāṇa' has no equivalent in the original texts. There is no such thing as 'entering into Nirvāṇa after death'. There is a word *parinibbuto* used to denote the death of the Buddha or an Arahant who has realized Nirvāṇa, but it does not mean 'entering into Nirvāṇa'. *Parinibbuto* simply means 'fully passed away', 'fully blown out' or 'fully extinct', because the Buddha or an Arahant has no re-existence after his death.

Now another question arises: What happens to the Buddha or an Arahant after his death, *parinirvāṇa*? This comes under the category of unanswered questions (*avyākata*).[3] Even when the Buddha spoke about this, he indicated that no words in our vocabulary could express what happens to an Arahant after his death. In reply to a Parivrājaka named Vaccha, the Buddha said that terms like 'born' or 'not born' do not apply in the case of an Arahant, because those things—matter, sensation, perception, mental activities, consciousness—with which the terms like 'born' and 'not born' are associated, are completely destroyed and uprooted, never to rise again after his death.[4]

An Arahant after his death is often compared to a fire gone out when the supply of wood is over, or to the flame of a lamp gone out when the wick and oil are finished.[5] Here it should

[1]S III (PTS), p. 189.
[2]There are some who write 'after the Nirvāṇa of the Buddha' instead of 'after the Parinirvāṇa of the Buddha'. 'After the Nirvāṇa of the Buddha' has no meaning, and the expression is unknown in Buddhist literature. It is always 'after the Parinirvāṇa of the Buddha'.
[3]S IV (PTS), p. 375 f.
[4]M I (PTS), p. 486.
[5]*Ibid.* I, p. 487; III, p. 245; Sn (PTS), v. 232 (p. 41).

be clearly and distinctly understood, without any confusion, that what is compared to a flame or a fire gone out is *not* Nirvāṇa, but the 'being' composed of the Five Aggregates who realized Nirvāṇa. This point has to be emphasized because many people, even some great scholars, have misunderstood and misinterpreted this simile as referring to Nirvāṇa. Nirvāṇa is never compared to a fire or a lamp gone out.

There is another popular question: If there is no Self, no *Ātman*, who realizes Nirvāṇa? Before we go on to Nirvāṇa, let us ask the question: Who thinks now, if there is no Self? We have seen earlier that it is the thought that thinks, that there is no thinker behind the thought. In the same way, it is wisdom (*paññā*), realization, that realizes. There is no other self behind the realization. In the discussion of the origin of *dukkha* we saw that whatever it may be—whether being, or thing, or system—if it is of the nature of arising, it has within itself the nature, the germ, of its cessation, its destruction. Now *dukkha*, *saṃsāra*, the cycle of continuity, is of the nature of arising; it must also be of the nature of cessation. *Dukkha* arises because of 'thirst' (*taṇhā*), and it ceases because of wisdom (*paññā*). 'Thirst' and wisdom are both within the Five Aggregates, as we saw earlier.[1]

Thus, the germ of their arising as well as that of their cessation are both within the Five Aggregates. This is the real meaning of the Buddha's well-known statement: 'Within this fathom-long sentient body itself, I postulate the world, the arising of the world, the cessation of the world, and the path leading to the cessation of the world.'[2] This means that all the Four Noble Truths are found within the Five Aggregates, i.e., within ourselves. (Here the word 'world' (*loka*) is used in place of *dukkha*). This also means that there is no external power that produces the arising and the cessation of *dukkha*.

When wisdom is developed and cultivated according to the Fourth Noble Truth (the next to be taken up), it sees the secret of life, the reality of things as they are. When the secret is discovered, when the Truth is seen, all the forces which feverishly produce the continuity of *saṃsāra* in illusion become calm and incapable of

---

[1]See Aggregate of Formations above pp. 22, 31.
[2]A (Colombo, 1929) p. 218.

producing any more karma-formations, because there is no more illusion, no more 'thirst' for continuity. It is like a mental disease which is cured when the cause or the secret of the malady is discovered and seen by the patient.

In almost all religions the *summum bonum* can be attained only after death. But Nirvāṇa can be realized in this very life; it is not necessary to wait till you die to 'attain' it.

He who has realized the Truth, Nirvāṇa, is the happiest being in the world. He is free from all 'complexes' and obsessions, the worries and troubles that torment others. His mental health is perfect. He does not repent the past, nor does he brood over the future. He lives fully in the present.[1] Therefore he appreciates and enjoys things in the purest sense without self-projections. He is joyful, exultant, enjoying the pure life, his faculties pleased, free from anxiety, serene and peaceful.[2] As he is free from selfish desire, hatred, ignorance, conceit, pride, and all such 'defilements', he is pure and gentle, full of universal love, compassion, kindness, sympathy, understanding and tolerance. His service to others is of the purest, for he has no thought of self. He gains nothing, accumulates nothing, not even anything spiritual, because he is free from the illusion of Self, and the 'thirst' for becoming.

Nirvāṇa is beyond all terms of duality and relativity. It is therefore beyond our conceptions of good and evil, right and wrong, existence and non-existence. Even the word 'happiness' (*sukha*) which is used to describe Nirvāṇa has an entirely different sense here. Sāriputta once said: 'O friend, Nirvāṇa is happiness! Nirvāṇa is happiness!' Then Udāyi asked: 'But, friend Sāriputta, what happiness can it be if there is no sensation?' Sāriputta's reply was highly philosophical and beyond ordinary comprehension: 'That there is no sensation itself is happiness'.

Nirvāṇa is beyond logic and reasoning (*atakkāvacara*). However much we may engage, often as a vain intellectual pastime, in highly speculative discussions regarding Nirvāṇa or Ultimate Truth or Reality, we shall never understand it that way. A child in the kindergarten should not quarrel about the theory of relativity. Instead, if he follows his studies patiently and diligently,

[1] S I (PTS), p. 5.
[2] M II (PTS), p. 121.

43

one day he may understand it. Nirvāṇa is 'to be realized by the wise within themselves' (*paccattaṃ veditabbo viññūhi*). If we follow the Path patiently and with diligence, train and purify ourselves earnestly, and attain the necessary spiritual development, we may one day realize it within ourselves—without taxing ourselves with puzzling and high-sounding words.

Let us therefore now turn to the Path which leads to the realization of Nirvāṇa.

CHAPTER V

THE FOURTH NOBLE TRUTH:

MAGGA: 'The Path'

The Fourth Noble Truth is that of the Way leading to the Cessation of *Dukkha* (*Dukkhanirodhagāminīpaṭipadā-ariyasacca*). This is known as the 'Middle Path' (*Majjhimā Paṭipadā*), because it avoids two extremes: one extreme being the search for happiness through the pleasures of the senses, which is 'low, common, unprofitable and the way of the ordinary people'; the other being the search for happiness through self-mortification in different forms of asceticism, which is 'painful, unworthy and unprofitable'. Having himself first tried these two extremes, and having found them to be useless, the Buddha discovered through personal experience the Middle Path 'which gives vision and knowledge, which leads to Calm, Insight, Enlightenment, Nirvāṇa'. This Middle Path is generally referred to as the Noble Eightfold Path (*Ariya-Aṭṭhaṅgika-Magga*), because it is composed of eight categories or divisions: namely,

1. Right Understanding (*Sammā diṭṭhi*),
2. Right Thought (*Sammā saṅkappa*),
3. Right Speech (*Sammā vācā*),
4. Right Action (*Sammā kammanta*),
5. Right Livelihood (*Sammā ājīva*),
6. Right Effort (*Sammā vāyāma*),
7. Right Mindfulness (*Sammā sati*),
8. Right Concentration (*Sammā samādhi*).

Practically the whole teaching of the Buddha, to which he devoted himself during 45 years, deals in some way or other with this Path. He explained it in different ways and in different words to different people, according to the stage of their development and their capacity to understand and follow him. But the essence of those many thousand discourses scattered in the Buddhist Scriptures is found in the Noble Eightfold Path.

It should not be thought that the eight categories or divisions of the Path should be followed and practised one after the other in the numerical order as given in the usual list above. But they are to be developed more or less simultaneously, as far as possible according to the capacity of each individual. They are all linked together and each helps the cultivation of the others.

These eight factors aim at promoting and perfecting the three essentials of Buddhist training and discipline: namely: (*a*) Ethical Conduct (*Sīla*), (*b*) Mental Discipline (*Samādhi*) and (*c*) Wisdom (*Paññā*).[1] It will therefore be more helpful for a coherent and better understanding of the eight divisions of the Path, if we group them and explain them according to these three heads.

Ethical Conduct (*Sīla*) is built on the vast conception of universal love and compassion for all living beings, on which the Buddha's teaching is based. It is regrettable that many scholars forget this great ideal of the Buddha's teaching, and indulge in only dry philosophical and metaphysical divagations when they talk and write about Buddhism. The Buddha gave his teaching 'for the good of the many, for the happiness of the many, out of compassion for the world' (*bahujanahitāya bahujanasukhāya lokānukampāya*).

According to Buddhism for a man to be perfect there are two qualities that he should develop equally: compassion (*karuṇā*) on one side, and wisdom (*paññā*) on the other. Here compassion represents love, charity, kindness, tolerance and such noble qualities on the emotional side, or qualities of the heart, while wisdom would stand for the intellectual side or the qualities of the mind. If one develops only the emotional neglecting the intellectual, one may become a good-hearted fool; while to develop only the intellectual side neglecting the emotional may turn one into a hard-hearted intellect without feeling for others. Therefore, to be perfect one has to develop both equally. That is the aim of the Buddhist way of life: in it wisdom and compassion are inseparably linked together, as we shall see later.

Now, in Ethical Conduct (*Sīla*), based on love and compassion,

[1] M I (PTS), p. 301.

46

are included three factors of the Noble Eightfold Path: namely, Right Speech, Right Action and Right Livelihood. (Nos. 3, 4 and 5 in the list).

Right speech means abstention (1) from telling lies, (2) from backbiting and slander and talk that may bring about hatred, enmity, disunity and disharmony among individuals or groups of people, (3) from harsh, rude, impolite, malicious and abusive language, and (4) from idle, useless and foolish babble and gossip. When one abstains from these forms of wrong and harmful speech one naturally has to speak the truth, has to use words that are friendly and benevolent, pleasant and gentle, meaningful and useful. One should not speak carelessly: speech should be at the right time and place. If one cannot say something useful, one should keep 'noble silence'.

Right Action aims at promoting moral, honourable and peaceful conduct. It admonishes us that we should abstain from destroying life, from stealing, from dishonest dealings, from illegitimate sexual intercourse, and that we should also help others to lead a peaceful and honourable life in the right way.

Right Livelihood means that one should abstain from making one's living through a profession that brings harm to others, such as trading in arms and lethal weapons, intoxicating drinks, poisons, killing animals, cheating, etc., and should live by a profession which is honourable, blameless and innocent of harm to others. One can clearly see here that Buddhism is strongly opposed to any kind of war, when it lays down that trade in arms and lethal weapons is an evil and unjust means of livelihood.

These three factors (Right Speech, Right Action and Right Livelihood) of the Eightfold Path constitute Ethical Conduct. It should be realized that the Buddhist ethical and moral conduct aims at promoting a happy and harmonious life both for the individual and for society. This moral conduct is considered as the indispensable foundation for all higher spiritual attainments. No spiritual development is possible without this moral basis.

Next comes Mental Discipline, in which are included three other factors of the Eightfold Path: namely, Right Effort, Right Mindfulness (or Attentiveness) and Right Concentration. (Nos. 6, 7 and 8 in the list).

Right Effort is the energetic will (1) to prevent evil and unwholesome states of mind from arising, and (2) to get rid of such evil and unwholesome states that have already arisen within a man, and also (3) to produce, to cause to arise, good and wholesome states of mind not yet arisen, and (4) to develop and bring to perfection the good and wholesome states of mind already present in a man.

Right Mindfulness (or Attentiveness) is to be diligently aware, mindful and attentive with regard to (1) the activities of the body (*kāya*), (2) sensations or feelings (*vedanā*), (3) the activities of the mind (*citta*) and (4) ideas, thoughts, conceptions and things (*dhamma*).

The practice of concentration on breathing (*ānāpānasati*) is one of the well-known exercises, connected with the body, for mental development. There are several other ways of developing attentiveness in relation to the body—as modes of meditation.

With regard to sensations and feelings, one should be clearly aware of all forms of feelings and sensations, pleasant, unpleasant and neutral, of how they appear and disappear within oneself.

Concerning the activities of mind, one should be aware whether one's mind is lustful or not, given to hatred or not, deluded or not, distracted or concentrated, etc. In this way one should be aware of all movements of mind, how they arise and disappear.

As regards ideas, thoughts, conceptions and things, one should know their nature, how they appear and disappear, how they are developed, how they are suppressed, and destroyed, and so on.

These four forms of mental culture or meditation are treated in detail in the *Satipaṭṭhāna-sutta* (Setting-up of Mindfulness).[1]

The third and last factor of Mental Discipline is Right Concentration leading to the four stages of *Dhyāna*, generally called trance or *recueillement*. In the first stage of *Dhyāna*, passionate desires and certain unwholesome thoughts like sensuous lust, ill-will, languor, worry, restlessness, and sceptical doubt are discarded, and feelings of joy and happiness are maintained, along with certain mental activities. In the second stage, all intellectual activities are suppressed, tranquillity and 'one-pointedness' of mind developed, and the feelings of joy and happiness are still

[1]See Chapter VII on Meditation.

48

The Buddha—from Tibet

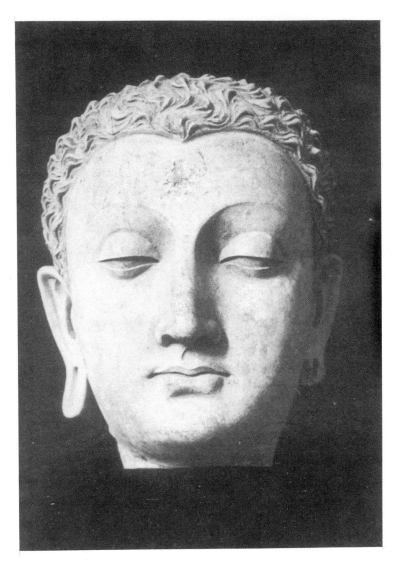

The head of the Buddha—from Afghanistan

The Buddha—from Cambodia

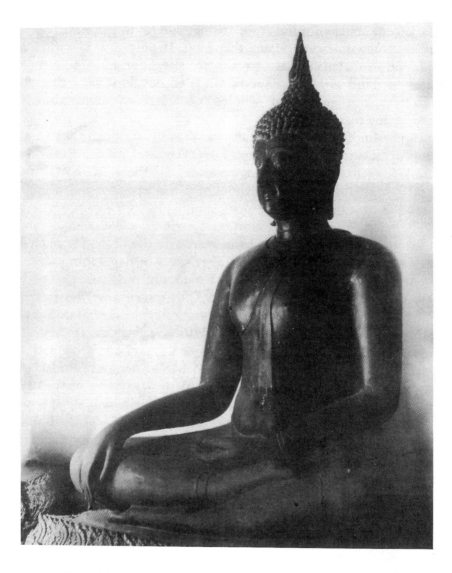

A Thai Buddha from the Golden Age of the Sukhothai period (17th century A.D.) is now in Wat Po (Temple of Reclining Buddha).

retained. In the third stage, the feeling of joy, which is an active sensation, also disappears, while the disposition of happiness still remains in addition to mindful equanimity. In the fourth stage of *Dhyāna*, all sensations, even of happiness and unhappiness, of joy and sorrow, disappear, only pure equanimity and awareness remaining.

Thus the mind is trained and disciplined and developed through Right Effort, Right Mindfulness, and Right Concentration.

The remaining two factors, namely Right Thought and Right Understanding go to constitute Wisdom.

Right Thought denotes the thoughts of selfless renunciation or detachment, thoughts of love and thoughts of non-violence, which are extended to all beings. It is very interesting and important to note here that thoughts of selfless detachment, love and non-violence are grouped on the side of wisdom. This clearly shows that true wisdom is endowed with these noble qualities, and that all thoughts of selfish desire, ill-will, hatred and violence are the result of a lack of wisdom—in all spheres of life whether individual, social, or political.

Right Understanding is the understanding of things as they are, and it is the Four Noble Truths that explain things as they really are. Right Understanding therefore is ultimately reduced to the understanding of the Four Noble Truths. This understanding is the highest wisdom which sees the Ultimate Reality. According to Buddhism there are two sorts of understanding: What we generally call understanding is knowledge, an accumulated memory, an intellectual grasping of a subject according to certain given data. This is called 'knowing accordingly' (*anubodha*). It is not very deep. Real deep understanding is called 'penetration' (*paṭivedha*), seeing a thing in its true nature, without name and label. This penetration is possible only when the mind is free from all impurities and is fully developed through meditation.[1]

From this brief account of the Path, one may see that it is a way of life to be followed, practised and developed by each individual. It is self-discipline in body, word and mind, self-development and self-purification. It has nothing to do with belief, prayer, worship or ceremony. In that sense, it has nothing

[1]Vism. (PTS), p. 510.

which may popularly be called 'religious'. It is a Path leading to the realization of Ultimate Reality, to complete freedom, happiness and peace through moral, spiritual and intellectual perfection.

In Buddhist countries there are simple and beautiful customs and ceremonies on religious occasions. They have little to do with the real Path. But they have their value in satisfying certain religious emotions and the needs of those who are less advanced, and helping them gradually along the Path.

With regard to the Four Noble Truths we have four functions to perform:

The First Noble Truth is *Dukkha*, the nature of life, its suffering, its sorrows and joys, its imperfection and unsatisfactoriness, its impermanence and insubstantiality. With regard to this, our function is to understand it as a fact, clearly and completely (*pariññeyya*).

The Second Noble Truth is the Origin of *Dukkha*, which is desire, 'thirst', accompanied by all other passions, defilements and impurities. A mere understanding of this fact is not sufficient. Here our function is to discard it, to eliminate, to destroy and eradicate it (*pahātabba*).

The Third Noble Truth is the Cessation of *Dukkha*, Nirvāṇa, the Absolute Truth, the Ultimate Reality. Here our function is to realize it (*sacchikātabba*).

The Fourth Noble Truth is the Path leading to the realization of Nirvāṇa. A mere knowledge of the Path, however complete, will not do. In this case, our function is to follow it and keep to it (*bhāvetabba*).[1]

[1]Mhvg. (Alutgama, 1922), p. 10.

CHAPTER VI

THE DOCTRINE OF NO-SOUL: *ANATTA*

What in general is suggested by Soul, Self, Ego, or to use the Sanskrit expression *Ātman*, is that in man there is a permanent, everlasting and absolute entity, which is the unchanging substance behind the changing phenomenal world. According to some religions, each individual has such a separate soul which is created by God, and which, finally after death, lives eternally either in hell or heaven, its destiny depending on the judgment of its creator. According to others, it goes through many lives till it is completely purified and becomes finally united with God or Brahman, Universal Soul or *Ātman*, from which it originally emanated. This soul or self in man is the thinker of thoughts, feeler of sensations, and receiver of rewards and punishments for all its actions good and bad. Such a conception is called the idea of self.

Buddhism stands unique in the history of human thought in denying the existence of such a Soul, Self, or *Ātman*. According to the teaching of the Buddha, the idea of self is an imaginary, false belief which has no corresponding reality, and it produces harmful thoughts of 'me' and 'mine', selfish desire, craving, attachment, hatred, ill-will, conceit, pride, egoism, and other defilements, impurities and problems. It is the source of all the troubles in the world from personal conflicts to wars between nations. In short, to this false view can be traced all the evil in the world.

Two ideas are psychologically deep-rooted in man: self-protection and self-preservation. For self-protection man has created God, on whom he depends for his own protection, safety and security, just as a child depends on its parent. For self-preservation man has conceived the idea of an immortal Soul or *Ātman*, which will live eternally. In his ignorance, weakness, fear, and desire, man needs these two things to console himself. Hence he clings to them deeply and fanatically.

The Buddha's teaching does not support this ignorance, weakness, fear, and desire, but aims at making man enlightened by removing and destroying them, striking at their very root. According to Buddhism, our ideas of God and Soul are false and empty. Though highly developed as theories, they are all the same extremely subtle mental projections, garbed in an intricate metaphysical and philosophical phraseology. These ideas are so deep-rooted in man, and so near and dear to him, that he does not wish to hear, nor does he want to understand, any teaching against them.

The Buddha knew this quite well. In fact, he said that his teaching was 'against the current' (*paṭisotagāmi*), against man's selfish desires. Just four weeks after his Enlightenment, seated under a banyan tree, he thought to himself: 'I have realized this Truth which is deep, difficult to see, difficult to understand . . . comprehensible only by the wise . . . Men who are overpowered by passions and surrounded by a mass of darkness cannot see this Truth, which is against the current, which is lofty, deep, subtle and hard to comprehend.'

With these thoughts in his mind, the Buddha hesitated for a moment, whether it would not be in vain if he tried to explain to the world the Truth he had just realized. Then he compared the world to a lotus pond: In a lotus pond there are some lotuses still under water; there are others which have risen only up to the water level; there are still others which stand above water and are untouched by it. In the same way in this world, there are men at different levels of development. Some would understand the Truth. So the Buddha decided to teach it.[1]

The doctrine of *Anatta* or No-Soul is the natural result of, or the corollary to, the analysis of the Five Aggregates and the teaching of Conditioned Genesis (*Paṭicca-samuppāda*).[2]

We have seen earlier, in the discussion of the First Noble Truth (*Dukkha*), that what we call a being or an individual is composed of the Five Aggregates, and that when these are analysed and examined, there is nothing behind them which can be taken as 'I', *Ātman*, or Self, or any unchanging abiding substance. That is the analytical method. The same result is arrived at through the

[1]Mhvg. (Alutgama, 1922), p. 4 f; M I (PTS), p. 167 f.
[2]Explained below.

doctrine of Conditioned Genesis which is the synthetical method, and according to this nothing in the world is absolute. Everything is conditioned, relative, and interdependent. This is the Buddhist theory of relativity.

Before we go into the question of *Anatta* proper, it is useful to have a brief idea of the Conditioned Genesis. The principle of this doctrine is given in a short formula of four lines:

When this is, that is (*Imasmiṃ sati idaṃ hoti*);
This arising, that arises (*Imassuppādā idaṃ uppajjati*);
When this is not, that is not (*Imasmiṃ asati idaṃ na hoti*);
This ceasing, that ceases (*Imassa nirodhā idaṃ nirujjhati*).[1]

On this principle of conditionality, relativity and interdependence, the whole existence and continuity of life and its cessation are explained in a detailed formula which is called *Paṭicca-samuppāda* 'Conditioned Genesis', consisting of twelve factors:

1. Through ignorance are conditioned volitional actions or karma-formations (*Avijjāpaccayā saṃkhārā*).
2. Through volitional actions is conditioned consciousness (*Saṃkhārapaccayā viññāṇaṃ*).
3. Through consciousness are conditioned mental and physical phenomena (*Viññāṇapaccayā nāmarūpaṃ*).
4. Through mental and physical phenomena are conditioned the six faculties (i.e., five physical sense-organs and mind) (*Nāmarūpapaccayā saḷāyatanaṃ*).
5. Through the six faculties is conditioned (sensorial and mental) contact (*Saḷāyatanapaccayā phasso*).
6. Through (sensorial and mental) contact is conditioned sensation (*Phassapaccayā vedanā*).
7. Through sensation is conditioned desire, 'thirst' (*Vedanāpaccayā taṇhā*).
8. Through desire ('thirst') is conditioned clinging (*Taṇhāpaccayā upādānaṃ*).

[1] M III (PTS), p. 63; S II (PTS), pp. 28, 95, etc. To put it into a modern form:
When A is, B is;
A arising, B arises;
When A is not, B is not;
A ceasing, B ceases.

9. Through clinging is conditioned the process of becoming (*Upādānapaccayā bhavo*).
10. Through the process of becoming is conditioned birth (*Bhavapaccayā jāti*).
11. Through birth are conditioned (12) decay, death, lamentation, pain, etc. (*Jātipaccayā jarāmaraṇaṃ . . .*).

This is how life arises, exists and continues. If we take this formula in reverse order, we come to the cessation of the process: Through the complete cessation of ignorance, volitional activities or karma-formations cease; through the cessation of volitional activities, consciousness ceases; . . . through the cessation of birth, decay, death, sorrow, etc., cease.

It should be remembered that each of these factors is conditioned (*paṭiccasamuppanna*) as well as conditioning (*paṭicca samuppāda*).[1] Therefore they are all relative, interdependent and interconnected, and nothing is absolute or independent; hence no first cause is accepted by Buddhism as we have seen earlier.[2] Conditioned Genesis should be considered as a circle, and not as a chain.[3]

The question of Free Will has occupied an important place in Western thought and philosophy. But according to Conditioned Genesis, this question does not and cannot arise in Buddhist philosophy. If the whole of existence is relative, conditioned and interdependent, how can will alone be free? Will which is included in the fourth Aggregate (*saṃkhārakkhandha*), like any other thought, is conditioned (*paṭicca-samuppanna*). So-called 'freedom' itself in this world is not absolutely free. That too is conditioned and relative. There is, of course, such a conditioned and relative 'Free Will', but not unconditioned and absolute. There can be nothing absolutely free in this world, physical or mental, as everything is conditioned and relative. If Free Will implies a will independent of conditions, independent of cause and effect, such a thing does not exist. How can a will, or anything for that matter, arise without conditions, away from cause and effect, when the whole of life, the whole of existence,

---

[1] Vism. (PTS), p. 517.
[2] See above p. 29.
[3] Limited space does not permit a discussion here of this most important doctrine. A critical and comparative study of this subject in detail will be found in a forthcoming work on Buddhist philosophy by the present writer.

CHAPTER VII

'MEDITATION' OR MENTAL CULTURE:

BHĀVANĀ

The Buddha said: 'O bhikkhus, there are two kinds of illness. What are those two? Physical illness and mental illness. There seem to be people who enjoy freedom from physical illness even for a year or two . . . even for a hundred years or more. But, O bhikkhus, rare in this world are those who enjoy freedom from mental illness even for one moment, except those who are free from mental defilements' (i.e., except arahants).[1]

The Buddha's teaching, particularly his way of 'meditation', aims at producing a state of perfect mental health, equilibrium and tranquility. It is unfortunate that hardly any other section of the Buddha's teaching is so much misunderstood as 'meditation', both by Buddhists and non-Buddhists. The moment the word 'meditation' is mentioned, one thinks of an escape from the daily activities of life; assuming a particular posture, like a statue in some cave or cell in a monastery, in some remote place cut off from society; and musing on, or being absorbed in, some kind of mystic or mysterious thought or trance. True Buddhist 'meditation' does not mean this kind of escape at all. The Buddha's teaching on this subject was so wrongly, or so little understood, that in later times the way of 'meditation' deteriorated and degenerated into a kind of ritual or ceremony almost technical in its routine.[2]

Most people are interested in meditation or *yoga* in order to gain some spiritual or mystic powers like the 'third eye', which others do not possess. There was some time ago a Buddhist nun in India who was trying to develop a power to see through her ears,

[1]A (Colombo, 1929), p. 276.
[2]*The Yogāvacara's Manual* (edited by T. W. Rhys Davids, London, 1896), a text on meditation written in Ceylon probably about the 18th century, shows how meditation at the time had degenerated into a ritual of reciting formulas, burning candles, etc.
See also Chapter XII on the Ascetic Ideal, *History of Buddhism in Ceylon* by Walpola Rahula, (Colombo, 1956), pp. 199 ff.

67

while she was still in the possession of the 'power' of perfect eyesight! This kind of idea is nothing but 'spiritual perversion'. It is always a question of desire, 'thirst' for power.

The word meditation is a very poor substitute for the original term *bhāvanā*, which means 'culture' or 'development', i.e., mental culture or mental development. The Buddhist *bhāvanā*, properly speaking, is mental culture in the full sense of the term. It aims at cleansing the mind of impurities and disturbances, such as lustful desires, hatred, ill-will, indolence, worries and restlessness, sceptical doubts, and cultivating such qualities as concentration, awareness, intelligence, will, energy, the analytical faculty, confidence, joy, tranquility, leading finally to the attainment of highest wisdom which sees the nature of things as they are, and realizes the Ultimate Truth, Nirvāṇa.

There are two forms of meditation. One is the development of mental concentration (*samatha* or *samādhi*), of one-pointedness of mind (*cittekaggatā*, Skt. *cittaikāgratā*), by various methods prescribed in the texts, leading up to the highest mystic states such as 'the Sphere of Nothingness' or 'the Sphere of Neither-Perception-nor-Non-Perception'. All these mystic states, according to the Buddha, are mind-created, mind-produced, conditioned (*saṃkhata*).[1] They have nothing to do with Reality, Truth, Nirvāṇa. This form of meditation existed before the Buddha. Hence it is not purely Buddhist, but it is not excluded from the field of Buddhist meditation. However it is not essential for the realization of Nirvāṇa. The Buddha himself, before his Enlightenment, studied these yogic practices under different teachers and attained to the highest mystic states; but he was not satisfied with them, because they did not give complete liberation, they did not give insight into the Ultimate Reality. He considered these mystic states only as 'happy living in this existence' (*diṭṭhadhammasukhavihāra*), or 'peaceful living' (*santavihāra*), and nothing more.[2]

He therefore discovered the other form of 'meditation' known as *vipassanā* (Skt. *vipaśyanā* or *vidarśanā*), 'Insight' into the nature of things, leading to the complete liberation of mind, to the realization of the Ultimate Truth, Nirvāṇa. This is essentially Buddhist

[1] See above p. 38.
[2] See *Sallekha-sutta* (no. 8), of M.

'meditation', Buddhist mental culture. It is an analytical method based on mindfulness, awareness, vigilance, observation.

It is impossible to do justice to such a vast subject in a few pages. However an attempt is made here to give a very brief and rough idea of the true Buddhist 'meditation', mental culture or mental development, in a practical way.

The most important discourse ever given by the Buddha on mental development ('meditation') is called the *Satipaṭṭhāna-sutta* 'The Setting-up of Mindfulness' (No. 22 of the *Dīgha-nikāya*, or No. 10 of the *Majjhima-nikāya*). This discourse is so highly venerated in tradition that it is regularly recited not only in Buddhist monasteries, but also in Buddhist homes with members of the family sitting round and listening with deep devotion. Very often bhikkhus recite this *sutta* by the bed-side of a dying man to purify his last thoughts.

The ways of 'meditation' given in this discourse are not cut off from life, nor do they avoid life; on the contrary, they are all connected with our life, our daily activities, our sorrows and joys, our words and thoughts, our moral and intellectual occupations.

The discourse is divided into four main sections: the first section deals with our body (*kāya*), the second with our feelings and sensations (*vedanā*), the third with the mind (*citta*), and the fourth with various moral and intellectual subjects (*dhamma*).

It should be clearly borne in mind that whatever the form of 'meditation' may be, the essential thing is mindfulness or awareness (*sati*), attention or observation (*anupassanā*).

One of the most well-known, popular and practical examples of 'meditation' connected with the body is called 'The Mindfulness or Awareness of in-and-out breathing' (*ānāpānasati*). It is for this 'meditation' only that a particular and definite posture is prescribed in the text. For other forms of 'meditation' given in this *sutta*, you may sit, stand, walk, or lie down, as you like. But, for cultivating mindfulness of in-and-out breathing, one should sit, according to the text, 'cross-legged, keeping the body erect and mindfulness alert'. But sitting cross-legged is not practical and easy for people of all countries, particularly for Westerners. Therefore, those who find it difficult to sit cross-legged, may sit on a chair, 'keeping the body erect and mindfulness alert'. It is very necessary for this exercise that the meditator should sit erect, but not stiff; his hands placed comfortably on his lap. Thus seated, you may close your eyes, or you may gaze at the tip of your nose, as it may be convenient to you.

You breathe in and out all day and night, but you are never mindful of it, you never for a second concentrate your mind on it. Now you are going to do just this. Breathe in and out as usual, without any effort or strain. Now, bring your mind to concentrate on your breathing-in and breathing-out; let your mind watch and observe your breathing in and out; let your mind be aware and vigilant of your breathing in and out. When you breathe, you sometimes take deep breaths, sometimes not. This does not matter at all. Breathe normally and naturally. The only thing is that when you take deep breaths you should be aware that they are deep breaths, and so on. In other words, your mind should be so fully concentrated on your breathing that you are aware of its movements and changes. Forget all other things, your surroundings, your environment; do not raise your eyes and look at anything. Try to do this for five or ten minutes.

At the beginning you will find it extremely difficult to bring your mind to concentrate on your breathing. You will be astonished how your mind runs away. It does not stay. You begin to think of various things. You hear sounds outside. Your mind is disturbed and distracted. You may be dismayed and disappointed. But if you continue to practise this exercise twice daily, morning and evening, for about five or ten minutes at a time, you will gradually, by and by, begin to concentrate your mind on your breathing. After a certain period, you will experience just that split second when your mind is fully concentrated on your breathing, when you will not hear even sounds nearby, when no external world exists for you. This slight moment is such a tremendous experience for you, full of joy, happiness and tranquility, that you would like to continue it. But still you cannot. Yet if you go on practising this regularly, you may repeat the experience again and again for longer and longer periods. That is the moment when you lose yourself completely in your mindfulness of breathing. As long as you are conscious of yourself you can never concentrate on anything.

This exercise of mindfulness of breathing, which is one of the simplest and easiest practices, is meant to develop concentration leading up to very high mystic attainments (*dhyāna*). Besides, the power of concentration is essential for any kind of deep understanding, penetration, insight into the nature of things, including the realization of Nirvāṇa.

Apart from all this, this exercise on breathing gives you immediate results. It is good for your physical health, for relaxation, sound sleep, and for efficiency in your daily work. It makes you calm and tranquil. Even at moments when you are nervous or excited, if you practise this for a couple of minutes, you will see for yourself that you become immediately quiet and at peace. You feel as if you have awakened after a good rest.

Another very important, practical, and useful form of 'meditation' (mental development) is to be aware and mindful of whatever you do, physically or verbally, during the daily routine of work in your life, private, public or professional. Whether you walk, stand, sit, lie down, or sleep, whether you stretch or bend your limbs, whether you look around, whether you put on your clothes, whether you talk or keep silence, whether you eat or drink, even whether you answer the calls of nature—in these and other activities, you should be fully aware and mindful of the act you perform at the moment. That is to say, that you should live in the present moment, in the present action. This does not mean that you should not think of the past or the future at all. On the contrary, you think of them in relation to the present moment, the present action, when and where it is relevant.

People do not generally live in their actions, in the present moment. They live in the past or in the future. Though they seem to be doing something now, here, they live somewhere else in their thoughts, in their imaginary problems and worries, usually in the memories of the past or in desires and speculations about the future. Therefore they do not live in, nor do they enjoy, what they do at the moment. So they are unhappy and discontented with the present moment, with the work at hand, and naturally they cannot give themselves fully to what they appear to be doing.

Sometimes you see a man in a restaurant reading while eating— a very common sight. He gives you the impression of being a very busy man, with no time even for eating. You wonder whether he eats or reads. One may say that he does both. In fact, he does neither, he enjoys neither. He is strained, and disturbed in mind,

71

and he does not enjoy what he does at the moment, does not live his life in the present moment, but unconsciously and foolishly tries to escape from life. (This does not mean, however, that one should not talk with a friend while having lunch or dinner.)

You cannot escape life however you may try. As long as you live, whether in a town or in a cave, you have to face it and live it. Real life is the present moment—not the memories of the past which is dead and gone, nor the dreams of the future which is not yet born. One who lives in the present moment lives the real life, and he is happiest.

When asked why his disciples, who lived a simple and quiet life with only one meal a day, were so radiant, the Buddha replied: 'They do not repent the past, nor do they brood over the future. They live in the present. Therefore they are radiant. By brooding over the future and repenting the past, fools dry up like green reeds cut down (in the sun).'[1]

Mindfulness, or awareness, does not mean that you should think and be conscious 'I am doing this' or 'I am doing that'. No. Just the contrary. The moment you think 'I am doing this', you become self-conscious, and then you do not live in the action, but you live in the idea 'I am', and consequently your work too is spoilt. You should forget yourself completely, and lose yourself in what you do. The moment a speaker becomes self-conscious and thinks 'I am addressing an audience', his speech is disturbed and his trend of thought broken. But when he forgets himself in his speech, in his subject, then he is at his best, he speaks well and explains things clearly. All great work—artistic, poetic, intellectual or spiritual—is produced at those moments when its creators are lost completely in their actions, when they forget themselves altogether, and are free from self-consciousness.

This mindfulness or awareness with regard to our activities, taught by the Buddha, is to live in the present moment, to live in the present action. (This is also the Zen way which is based primarily on this teaching.) Here in this form of meditation, you haven't got to perform any particular action in order to develop mindfulness, but you have only to be mindful and aware of whatever you may do. You haven't got to spend one second of

[1] S I (PTS), p. 5.

72

your precious time on this particular 'meditation': you have only to cultivate mindfulness and awareness always, day and night, with regard to all activities in your usual daily life. These two forms of 'meditation' discussed above are connected with our body.

Then there is a way of practising mental development ('meditation') with regard to all our sensations or feelings, whether happy, unhappy or neutral. Let us take only one example. You experience an unhappy, sorrowful sensation. In this state your mind is cloudy, hazy, not clear, it is depressed. In some cases, you do not even see clearly why you have that unhappy feeling. First of all, you should learn not to be unhappy about your unhappy feeling, not to be worried about your worries. But try to see clearly why there is a sensation or a feeling of unhappiness, or worry, or sorrow. Try to examine how it arises, its cause, how it disappears, its cessation. Try to examine it as if you are observing it from outside, without any subjective reaction, as a scientist observes some object. Here, too, you should not look at it as 'my feeling' or 'my sensation' subjectively, but only look at it as 'a feeling' or 'a sensation' objectively. You should forget again the false idea of 'I'. When you see its nature, how it arises and disappears, your mind grows dispassionate towards that sensation, and becomes detached and free. It is the same with regard to all sensations or feelings.

Now let us discuss the form of 'meditation' with regard to our minds. You should be fully aware of the fact whenever your mind is passionate or detached, whenever it is overpowered by hatred, ill-will, jealousy, or is full of love, compassion, whenever it is deluded or has a clear and right understanding, and so on and so forth. We must admit that very often we are afraid or ashamed to look at our own minds. So we prefer to avoid it. One should be bold and sincere and look at one's own mind as one looks at one's face in a mirror.[1]

Here is no attitude of criticizing or judging, or discriminating between right and wrong, or good and bad. It is simply observing, watching, examining. You are not a judge, but a scientist. When you observe your mind, and see its true nature clearly, you become dispassionate with regard to its emotions, sentiments and states.

[1] M I (PTS), p. 100.

73

Thus you become detached and free, so that you may see things as they are.

Let us take one example. Say you are really angry, overpowered by anger, ill-will, hatred. It is curious, and paradoxical, that the man who is in anger is not really aware, not mindful that he is angry. The moment he becomes aware and mindful of that state of his mind, the moment he sees his anger, it becomes, as if it were, shy and ashamed, and begins to subside. You should examine its nature, how it arises, how it disappears. Here again it should be remembered that you should not think 'I am angry', or of 'my anger'. You should only be aware and mindful of the state of an angry mind. You are only observing and examining an angry mind objectively. This should be the attitude with regard to all sentiments, emotions, and states of mind.

Then there is a form of 'meditation' on ethical, spiritual and intellectual subjects. All our studies, reading, discussions, conversation and deliberations on such subjects are included in this 'meditation'. To read this book, and to think deeply about the subjects discussed in it, is a form of meditation. We have seen earlier[1] that the conversation between Khemaka and the group of monks was a form of meditation which led to the realization of Nirvāṇa.

So, according to this form of meditation, you may study, think, and deliberate on the Five Hindrances (*Nīvaraṇa*), namely:

1. lustful desires (*kāmacchanda*),
2. ill-will, hatred or anger (*vyāpāda*),
3. torpor and languor (*thīna-middha*),
4. restlessness and worry (*uddhacca-kukkucca*),
5. sceptical doubts (*vicikicchā*).

These five are considered as hindrances to any kind of clear understanding, as a matter of fact, to any kind of progress. When one is over-powered by them and when one does not know how to get rid of them, then one cannot understand right and wrong, or good and bad.

One may also 'meditate' on the Seven Factors of Enlightenment (*Bojjhaṅga*). They are:

[1]See above p. 65.

74

1. Mindfulness (*sati*), i.e., to be aware and mindful in all activities and movements both physical and mental, as we discussed above.

2. Investigation and research into the various problems of doctrine (*dhamma-vicaya*). Included here are all our religious, ethical and philosophical studies, reading, researches, discussions, conversation, even attending lectures relating to such doctrinal subjects.

3. Energy (*viriya*), to work with determination till the end.

4. Joy (*pīti*), the quality quite contrary to the pessimistic, gloomy or melancholic attitude of mind.

5. Relaxation (*passaddhi*) of both body and mind. One should not be stiff physically or mentally.

6. Concentration (*samādhi*), as discussed above.

7. Equanimity (*upekkhā*), i.e., to be able to face life in all its vicissitudes with calm of mind, tranquillity, without disturbance.

To cultivate these qualities the most essential thing is a genuine wish, will, or inclination. Many other material and spiritual conditions conducive to the development of each quality are described in the texts.

One may also 'meditate' on such subjects as the Five Aggregates investigating the question 'What is a being?' or 'What is it that is called I?', or on the Four Noble Truths, as we discussed above. Study and investigation of those subjects constitute this fourth form of meditation, which leads to the realization of Ultimate Truth.

Apart from those we have discussed here, there are many other subjects of meditation, traditionally forty in number, among which mention should be made particularly of the four Sublime States: (*Brahma-vihāra*): (1) extending unlimited, universal love and good-will (*mettā*) to all living beings without any kind of discrimination, 'just as a mother loves her only child'; (2) compassion (*karuṇā*) for all living beings who are suffering, in trouble and affliction; (3) sympathetic joy (*muditā*) in others' success, welfare and happiness; and (4) equanimity (*upekkhā*) in all vicissitudes of life.

75

CHAPTER VIII

WHAT THE BUDDHA TAUGHT AND

THE WORLD TODAY

There are some who believe that Buddhism is so lofty and sublime a system that it cannot be practised by ordinary men and women in this workaday world of ours, and that one has to retire from it to a monastery, or to some quiet place, if one desires to be a true Buddhist.

This is a sad misconception, due evidently to a lack of understanding of the teaching of the Buddha. People run to such hasty and wrong conclusions as a result of their hearing, or reading casually, something about Buddhism written by someone, who, as he has not understood the subject in all its aspects, gives only a partial and lopsided view of it. The Buddha's teaching is meant not only for monks in monasteries, but also for ordinary men and women living at home with their families. The Noble Eightfold Path, which is the Buddhist way of life, is meant for all, without distinction of any kind.

The vast majority of people in the world cannot turn monk, or retire into caves or forests. However noble and pure Buddhism may be, it would be useless to the masses of mankind if they could not follow it in their daily life in the world of today. But if you understand the spirit of Buddhism correctly (and not only its letter), you can surely follow and practise it while living the life of an ordinary man.

There may be some who find it easier and more convenient to accept Buddhism, if they do live in a remote place, cut off from the society of others. Others may find that that kind of retirement dulls and depresses their whole being both physically and mentally, and that it may not therefore be conducive to the development of their spiritual and intellectual life.

True renunciation does not mean running away physically from the world. Sāriputta, the chief disciple of the Buddha, said that one man might live in a forest devoting himself to ascetic practices, but might be full of impure thoughts and 'defilements'; another might live in a village or a town, practising no ascetic discipline, but his mind might be pure, and free from 'defilements'. Of these two, said Sāriputta, the one who lives a pure life in the village or town is definitely far superior to, and greater than, the one who lives in the forest.[1]

The common belief that to follow the Buddha's teaching one has to retire from life is a misconception. It is really an unconscious defence against practising it. There are numerous references in Buddhist literature to men and women living ordinary, normal family lives who successfully practised what the Buddha taught, and realized Nirvāṇa. Vacchagotta the Wanderer, (whom we met earlier in the chapter on *Anatta*), once asked the Buddha straightforwardly whether there were laymen and women leading the family life, who followed his teaching successfully and attained to high spiritual states. The Buddha categorically stated that there were not one or two, not a hundred or two hundred or five hundred, but many more laymen and women leading the family life who followed his teaching successfully and attained to high spiritual states.[2]

It may be agreeable for certain people to live a retired life in a quiet place away from noise and disturbance. But it is certainly more praiseworthy and courageous to practise Buddhism living among your fellow beings, helping them and being of service to them. It may perhaps be useful in some cases for a man to live in retirement for a time in order to improve his mind and character, as preliminary moral, spiritual and intellectual training, to be strong enough to come out later and help others. But if a man lives all his life in solitude, thinking only of his own happiness and 'salvation', without caring for his fellows, this surely is not in keeping with the Buddha's teaching which is based on love, compassion, and service to others.

One might now ask: If a man can follow Buddhism while living the life of an ordinary layman, why was the Sangha, the Order of monks, established by the Buddha? The Order provides opportunity for those who are willing to devote their lives not

[1] M I (PTS), pp. 30-31.
[2] *Ibid.*, pp. 490 ff.

77

only to their own spiritual and intellectual development, but also to the service of others. An ordinary layman with a family cannot be expected to devote his whole life to the service of others, whereas a monk, who has no family responsibilities or any other worldly ties, is in a position to devote his whole life 'for the good of the many, for the happiness of the many' according to the Buddha's advice. That is how in the course of history, the Buddhist monastery became not only a spiritual centre, but also a centre of learning and culture.

The *Sigāla-sutta* (No. 31 of the *Dīgha-nikāya*) shows with what great respect the layman's life, his family and social relations are regarded by the Buddha.

A young man named Sigāla used to worship the six cardinal points of the heavens—east, south, west, north, nadir and zenith— in obeying and observing the last advice given him by his dying father. The Buddha told the young man that in the 'noble discipline' (*ariyassa vinaye*) of his teaching the six directions were different. According to his 'noble discipline' the six directions were: east: parents; south: teachers; west: wife and children; north: friends, relatives and neighbours; nadir: servants, workers and employees; zenith: religious men.

'One should worship these six directions' said the Buddha. Here the word 'worship' (*namasseyya*) is very significant, for one worships something sacred, something worthy of honour and respect. These six family and social groups mentioned above are treated in Buddhism as sacred, worthy of respect and worship. But how is one to 'worship' them? The Buddha says that one could 'worship' them only by performing one's duties towards them. These duties are explained in his discourse to Sigāla.

First: Parents are sacred to their children. The Buddha says: 'Parents are called Brahma' (*Brahmāti mātāpitaro*). The term *Brahma* denotes the highest and most sacred conception in Indian thought, and in it the Buddha includes parents. So in good Buddhist families at the present time children literally 'worship' their parents every day, morning and evening. They have to perform certain duties towards their parents according to the 'noble discipline': they should look after their parents in their old age; should do whatever they have to do on their behalf; should maintain the honour of the family and continue the family tradition;

78

should protect the wealth earned by their parents; and perform their funeral rites after their death. Parents, in their turn, have certain responsibilities towards their children: they should keep their children away from evil courses; should engage them in good and profitable activities; should give them a good education; should marry them into good families; and should hand over the property to them in due course.

Second: The relation between teacher and pupil: a pupil should respect and be obedient to his teacher; should attend to his needs if any; should study earnestly. And the teacher, in his turn, should train and shape his pupil properly; should teach him well; should introduce him to his friends; and should try to procure him security or employment when his education is over.

Third: The relation between husband and wife: love between husband and wife is considered almost religious or sacred. It is called *sadāra-Brahmacariya* 'sacred family life'. Here, too, the significance of the term *Brahma* should be noted: the highest respect is given to this relationship. Wives and husbands should be faithful, respectful and devoted to each other, and they have certain duties towards each other: the husband should always honour his wife and never be wanting in respect to her; he should love her and be faithful to her; should secure her position and comfort; and should please her by presenting her with clothing and jewellery. (The fact that the Buddha did not forget to mention even such a thing as the gifts a husband should make to his wife shows how understanding and sympathetic were his humane feelings towards ordinary human emotions.) The wife, in her turn, should supervise and look after household affairs; should entertain guests, visitors, friends, relatives and employees; should love and be faithful to her husband; should protect his earnings; should be clever and energetic in all activities.

Fourth: The relation between friends, relatives and neighbours: they should be hospitable and charitable to one another; should speak pleasantly and agreeably; should work for each other's welfare; should be on equal terms with one another; should not quarrel among themselves; should help each other in need; and should not forsake each other in difficulty.

Fifth: The relation between master and servant: the master or the employer has several obligations towards his servant or his

79

employee: work should be assigned according to ability and capacity; adequate wages should be paid; medical needs should be provided; occasional donations or bonuses should be granted. The servant or employee, in his turn, should be diligent and not lazy; honest and obedient and not cheat his master; he should be earnest in his work.

Sixth: The relation between the religious (lit. recluses and brāhmaṇas) and the laity: lay people should look after the material needs of the religious with love and respect; the religious with a loving heart should impart knowledge and learning to the laity, and lead them along the good path away from evil.

We see then that the lay life, with its family and social relations, is included in the 'noble discipline', and is within the framework of the Buddhist way of life, as the Buddha envisaged it.

So in the *Saṃyutta-nikāya*, one of the oldest Pali texts, Sakka, the king of the gods (*devas*), declares that he worships not only the monks who live a virtuous holy life, but also 'lay disciples (*upāsaka*) who perform meritorious deeds, who are virtuous, and maintain their families righteously'.[1]

If one desires to become a Buddhist, there is no initiation ceremony (or baptism) which one has to undergo. (But to become a *bhikkhu*, a member of the Order of the *Sangha*, one has to undergo a long process of disciplinary training and education.) If one understands the Buddha's teaching, and if one is convinced that his teaching is the right Path and if one tries to follow it, then one is a Buddhist. But according to the unbroken age-old tradition in Buddhist countries, one is considered a Buddhist if one takes the Buddha, the *Dhamma* (the Teaching) and the *Sangha* (the Order of Monks)—generally called 'the Triple-Gem'—as one's refuges, and undertakes to observe the Five Precepts (*Pañca-sīla*)—the minimum moral obligations of a lay Buddhist—(1) not to destroy life, (2) not to steal, (3) not to commit adultery, (4) not to tell lies, (5) not to take intoxicating drinks—reciting the formulas given in the ancient texts. On religious occasions Buddhists in congregation usually recite these formulas, following the lead of a Buddhist monk.

There are no external rites or ceremonies which a Buddhist has

[1] S I (PTS), p. 234.

The Buddha—from Anurādhapura, Sri Lanka

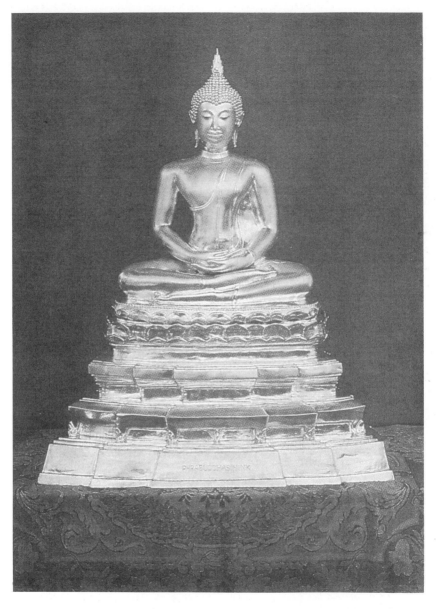

Phra Buddha Sihink of the Buddhapadipa Temple 14 Calonne Rood, Wimbledon, in London is a replica of the original in the Royal Hall, National Museum, Bangkok, 1988 (2531 B.E.)

to perform. Buddhism is a way of life, and what is essential is following the Noble Eightfold Path. Of course there are in all Buddhist countries simple and beautiful ceremonies on religious occasions. There are shrines with statues of the Buddha, *stūpas* or *dāgäbas* and Bo-trees in monasteries where Buddhists worship, offer flowers, light lamps and burn incense. This should not be likened to prayer in theistic religions; it is only a way of paying homage to the memory of the Master who showed the way. These traditional observances, though inessential, have their value in satisfying the religious emotions and needs of those who are less advanced intellectually and spiritually, and helping them gradually along the Path.

Those who think that Buddhism is interested only in lofty ideals, high moral and philosophical thought, and that it ignores the social and economic welfare of people, are wrong. The Buddha was interested in the happiness of men. To him happiness was not possible without leading a pure life based on moral and spiritual principles. But he knew that leading such a life was hard in unfavourable material and social conditions.

Buddhism does not consider material welfare as an end in itself: it is only a means to an end—a higher and nobler end. But it is a means which is indispensable, indispensable in achieving a higher purpose for man's happiness. So Buddhism recognizes the need of certain minimum material conditions favourable to spiritual success—even that of a monk engaged in meditation in some solitary place.[1]

The Buddha did not take life out of the context of its social and economic background; he looked at it as a whole, in all its social, economic and political aspects. His teachings on ethical, spiritual and philosophical problems are fairly well known. But little is known, particularly in the West, about his teaching on social, economic and political matters. Yet there are numerous discourses dealing with these scattered throughout the ancient Buddhist texts. Let us take only a few examples.

The *Cakkavattisīhanāda-sutta* of the *Dīgha-nikāya* (No. 26) clearly states that poverty (*dāliddiya*) is the cause of immorality and crimes

[1]MA I (PTS), p. 290 f. (Buddhist monks, members of the order of the *Sangha*, are not expected to have personal property, but they are allowed to hold communal (*Sanghika*) property).

81

such as theft, falsehood, violence, hatred, cruelty, etc. Kings in ancient times, like governments today, tried to suppress crime through punishment. The *Kūṭadanta-sutta* of the same *Nikāya* explains how futile this is. It says that this method can never be successful. Instead the Buddha suggests that, in order to eradicate crime, the economic condition of the people should be improved: grain and other facilities for agriculture should be provided for farmers and cultivators; capital should be provided for traders and those engaged in business; adequate wages should be paid to those who are employed. When people are thus provided for with opportunities for earning a sufficient income, they will be contented, will have no fear or anxiety, and consequently the country will be peaceful and free from crime.[1]

Because of this, the Buddha told lay people how important it is to improve their economic condition. This does not mean that he approved of hoarding wealth with desire and attachment, which is against his fundamental teaching, nor did he approve of each and every way of earning one's livelihood. There are certain trades like the production and sale of armaments, which he condemns as evil means of livelihood, as we saw earlier.[2]

A man named Dīghajānu once visited the Buddha and said: 'Venerable Sir, we are ordinary lay men, leading the family life with wife and children. Would the Blessed One teach us some doctrines which will be conducive to our happiness in this world and hereafter.'

The Buddha tells him that there are four things which are conducive to a man's happiness in this world: First: he should be skilled, efficient, earnest, and energetic in whatever profession he is engaged, and he should know it well (*uṭṭhāna-sampadā*); second: he should protect his income, which he has thus earned righteously, with the sweat of his brow (*ārakkha-sampadā*); (This refers to protecting wealth from thieves, etc. All these ideas should be considered against the background of the period.) third: he should have good friends (*kalyāṇa-mitta*) who are faithful, learned, virtuous, liberal and intelligent, who will help him along the right path away from evil; fourth: he should spend reasonably, in proportion to his income, neither too much nor too little,

[1] D I (Colombo, 1929), p. 101.
[2] See above p. 47.

82

i.e., he should not hoard wealth avariciously, nor should he be extravagant—in other words he should live within his means (*samajivikatā*).

Then the Buddha expounds the four virtues conducive to a layman's happiness hereafter: (1) *Saddhā*: he should have faith and confidence in moral, spiritual and intellectual values; (2) *Sīla*: he should abstain from destroying and harming life, from stealing and cheating, from adultery, from falsehood, and from intoxicating drinks; (3) *Cāga*: he should practise charity, generosity, without attachment and craving for his wealth; (4) *Paññā*: he should develop wisdom which leads to the complete destruction of suffering, to the realization of Nirvāṇa.[1]

Sometimes the Buddha even went into details about saving money and spending it, as, for instance, when he told the young man Sigāla that he should spend one fourth of his income on his daily expenses, invest half in his business and put aside one fourth for any emergency.[2]

Once the Buddha told Anāthapiṇḍika, the great banker, one of his most devoted lay disciples who founded for him the celebrated Jetavana monastery at Sāvatthi, that a layman, who leads an ordinary family life, has four kinds of happiness. The first happiness is to enjoy economic security or sufficient wealth acquired by just and righteous means (*atthi-sukha*); the second is spending that wealth liberally on himself, his family, his friends and relatives, and on meritorious deeds (*bhoga-sukha*); the third to be free from debts (*anaṇa-sukha*); the fourth happiness is to live a faultless, and a pure life without committing evil in thought, word or deed (*anavajja-sukha*). It must be noted here that three of these kinds are economic, and that the Buddha finally reminded the banker that economic and material happiness is 'not worth one sixteenth part' of the spiritual happiness arising out of a faultless and good life.[3]

From the few examples given above, one could see that the Buddha considered economic welfare as requisite for human happiness, but that he did not recognize progress as real and true

---

[1]A (Colombo, 1929), pp. 786 ff.
[2]D III (Colombo, 1929), p. 115.
[3]A (Colombo, 1929), pp. 232-233.

if it was only material, devoid of a spiritual and moral foundation. While encouraging material progress, Buddhism always lays great stress on the development of the moral and spiritual character for a happy, peaceful and contented society.

The Buddha was just as clear on politics, on war and peace. It is too well known to be repeated here that Buddhism advocates and preaches non-violence and peace as its universal message, and does not approve of any kind of violence or destruction of life. According to Buddhism there is nothing that can be called a 'just war'—which is only a false term coined and put into circulation to justify and excuse hatred, cruelty, violence and massacre. Who decides what is just or unjust? The mighty and the victorious are 'just', and the weak and the defeated are 'unjust'. Our war is always 'just', and your war is always 'unjust'. Buddhism does not accept this position.

The Buddha not only taught non-violence and peace, but he even went to the field of battle itself and intervened personally, and prevented war, as in the case of the dispute between the Sākyas and the Koliyas, who were prepared to fight over the question of the waters of the Rohini. And his words once prevented King Ajātasattu from attacking the kingdom of the Vajjis.

In the days of the Buddha, as today, there were rulers who governed their countries unjustly. People were oppressed and exploited, tortured and persecuted, excessive taxes were imposed and cruel punishments were inflicted. The Buddha was deeply moved by these inhumanities. The *Dhammapadaṭṭhakathā* records that he, therefore, directed his attention to the problem of good government. His views should be appreciated against the social, economic and political background of his time. He had shown how a whole country could become corrupt, degenerate and unhappy when the heads of its government, that is the king, the ministers and administrative officers become corrupt and unjust. For a country to be happy it must have a just government. How this form of just government could be realized is explained by the Buddha in his teaching of the 'Ten Duties of the King' (*dasa-rāja-dhamma*), as given in the *Jātaka* text.[1]

Of course the term 'king' (*Rāja*) of old should be replaced today

[1] Jataka I, 260, 399; II, 400; III, 274, 320; V, 119, 378.

84

by the term 'Government'. 'The Ten Duties of the King', therefore, apply today to all those who constitute the government, such as the head of the state, ministers, political leaders, legislative and administrative officers, etc.

The first of the 'Ten Duties of the King' is liberality, generosity, charity (*dāna*). The ruler should not have craving and attachment to wealth and property, but should give it away for the welfare of the people.

Second: A high moral character (*sīla*). He should never destroy life, cheat, steal and exploit others, commit adultery, utter falsehood, and take intoxicating drinks. That is, he must at least observe the Five Precepts of the layman.

Third: Sacrificing everything for the good of the people (*pariccāga*), he must be prepared to give up all personal comfort, name and fame, and even his life, in the interest of the people.

Fourth: Honesty and integrity (*ajjava*). He must be free from fear or favour in the discharge of his duties, must be sincere in his intentions, and must not deceive the public.

Fifth: Kindness and gentleness (*maddava*). He must possess a genial temperament.

Sixth: Austerity in habits (*tapa*). He must lead a simple life, and should not indulge in a life of luxury. He must have self-control.

Seventh: Freedom from hatred, ill-will, enmity (*akkodha*). He should bear no grudge against anybody.

Eighth: Non-violence (*avihiṃsā*), which means not only that he should harm nobody, but also that he should try to promote peace by avoiding and preventing war, and everything which involves violence and destruction of life.

Ninth: Patience, forbearance, tolerance, understanding (*khanti*). He must be able to bear hardships, difficulties and insults without losing his temper.

Tenth: Non-opposition, non-obstruction (*avirodha*), that is to say that he should not oppose the will of the people, should not obstruct any measures that are conducive to the welfare of the people. In other words he should rule in harmony with his people.[1]

[1]It is interesting to note here that the Five Principles or *Pancha-sīla* in India's foreign policy are in accordance with the Buddhist principles which Asoka, the great Buddhist emperor of India, applied to the administration of his government in the 3rd century B.C. The expression *Pancha-sīla* (Five Precepts or Virtues), is itself a Buddhist term.

If a country is ruled by men endowed with such qualities, it is needless to say that that country must be happy. But this was not a Utopia, for there were kings in the past like Asoka of India who had established kingdoms based on these ideas.

The world today lives in constant fear, suspicion, and tension. Science has produced weapons which are capable of unimaginable destruction. Brandishing these new instruments of death, great powers threaten and challenge one another, boasting shamelessly that one could cause more destruction and misery in the world than the other.

They have gone along this path of madness to such a point that, now, if they take one more step forward in that direction, the result will be nothing but mutual annihilation along with the total destruction of humanity.

Human beings in fear of the situation they have themselves created, want to find a way out, and seek some kind of solution. But there is none except that held out by the Buddha—his message of non-violence and peace, of love and compassion, of tolerance and understanding, of truth and wisdom, of respect and regard for all life, of freedom from selfishness, hatred and violence.

The Buddha says: 'Never by hatred is hatred appeased, but it is appeased by kindness. This is an eternal truth.'[1]

'One should win anger through kindness, wickedness through goodness, selfishness through charity, and falsehood through truthfulness.'[2]

There can be no peace or happiness for man as long as he desires and thirsts after conquering and subjugating his neighbour. As the Buddha says: 'The victor breeds hatred, and the defeated lies down in misery. He who renounces both victory and defeat is happy and peaceful.'[3] The only conquest that brings peace and happiness is self-conquest. 'One may conquer millions in battle, but he who conquers himself, only one, is the greatest of conquerors.'[4]

You will say this is all very beautiful, noble and sublime, but impractical. Is it practical to hate one another? To kill one

[1]Dhp. I 5.
[2]*Ibid.* XVII 3.
[3]*Ibid.* XV 5.
[4]*Ibid.* VIII 4.

another? To live in eternal fear and suspicion like wild animals in a jungle? Is this more practical and comfortable? Was hatred ever appeased by hatred? Was evil ever won over by evil? But there are examples, at least in individual cases, where hatred is appeased by love and kindness, and evil won over by goodness. You will say that this may be true, practicable in individual cases, but that it never works in national and international affairs. People are hypnotized, psychologically puzzled, blinded and deceived by the political and propaganda usage of such terms as 'national', 'international', or 'state'. What is a nation but a vast conglomeration of individuals? A nation or a state does not act, it is the individual who acts. What the individual thinks and does is what the nation or the state thinks and does. What is applicable to the individual is applicable to the nation or the state. If hatred can be appeased by love and kindness on the individual scale, surely it can be realized on the national and international scale too. Even in the case of a single person, to meet hatred with kindness one must have tremendous courage, boldness, faith and confidence in moral force. May it not be even more so with regard to international affairs? If by the expression 'not practical' you mean 'not easy', you are right. Definitely it is not easy. Yet it should be tried. You may say it is risky trying it. Surely it cannot be more risky than trying a nuclear war.

It is a consolation and inspiration to think today that at least there was one great ruler, well known in history, who had the courage, the confidence and the vision to apply this teaching of non-violence, peace and love to the administration of a vast empire, in both internal and external affairs—Asoka, the great Buddhist emperor of India (3rd century B.C.)—'the Beloved of the gods' as he was called.

At first he followed the example of his father (Bindusāra) and grandfather (Chandragupta), and wished to complete the conquest of the Indian peninsula. He invaded and conquered Kalinga, and annexed it. Many hundreds of thousands were killed, wounded, tortured and taken prisoner in this war. But later, when he became a Buddhist, he was completely changed and transformed by the Buddha's teachings. In one of his famous Edicts, inscribed on rock, (Rock Edict XIII, as it is now called), the original of which one may read even today, referring to the conquest of Kalinga, the

Emperor publicly expressed his 'repentance', and said how 'extremely painful' it was for him to think of that carnage. He publicly declared that he would never draw his sword again for any conquest, but that he 'wishes all living beings non-violence, self control, the practice of serenity and mildness. This, of course, is considered the chief conquest by the Beloved of the gods (i.e., Asoka), namely the conquest by piety (*dhamma-vijaya*).' Not only did he renounce war himself, he expressed his desire that 'my sons and grandsons will not think of a new conquest as worth achieving . . . let them think of that conquest only which is the conquest by piety. That is good for this world and the world beyond.'

This is the only example in the history of mankind of a victorious conquerer at the zenith of his power, still possessing the strength to continue his territorial conquests, yet renouncing war and violence and turning to peace and non-violence.

Here is a lesson for the world today. The ruler of an empire publicly turned his back on war and violence and embraced the message of peace and non-violence. There is no historical evidence to show that any neighbouring king took advantage of Asoka's piety to attack him militarily, or that there was any revolt or rebellion within his empire during his lifetime. On the contrary there was peace throughout the land, and even countries outside his empire seem to have accepted his benign leadership.

To talk of maintaining peace through the balance of power, or through the threat of nuclear deterrents, is foolish. The might of armaments can only produce fear, and not peace. It is impossible that there can be genuine and lasting peace through fear. Through fear can come only hatred, ill-will and hostility, suppressed perhaps for the time being only, but ready to erupt and become violent at any moment. True and genuine peace can prevail only in an atmosphere of *mettā*, amity, free from fear, suspicion and danger.

Buddhism aims at creating a society where the ruinous struggle for power is renounced; where calm and peace prevail away from conquest and defeat; where the persecution of the innocent is vehemently denounced; where one who conquers oneself is more respected than those who conquer millions by military and economic warfare; where hatred is conquered by kindness, and evil by goodness; where enmity, jealousy, ill-will and greed do not infect

88

men's minds; where compassion is the driving force of action; where all, including the least of living things, are treated with fairness, consideration and love; where life in peace and harmony, in a world of material contentment, is directed towards the highest and noblest aim, the realization of the Ultimate Truth, Nirvāṇa.

Selected Texts

A word of explanation may help the modern reader to understand and appreciate the style of the original Pali texts selected for translation here.

Three months after the Buddha's *Parinirvāṇa* (death), a Council of the disciples closely associated with him was held, at which all his teaching, discourses and rules of discipline, as they were remembered, were recited, approved as authentic, and classified into five Collections, called *Nikāyas*, which constitute the *Tipiṭaka* (Triple Canon). These Collections were entrusted to various Theras or Elders and to their pupilary succession for oral transmission for the benefit of future generations.

In order to perpetuate an unbroken and authentic oral transmission, regular and systematic recitation is necessary. It must be particularly noted that this recitation was not the act of a single individual alone, but of a group. The purpose of this mode of collective recitation was to keep the texts intact, free from change, modification or interpolation. If one member of the group forgot a word, another would remember it; or if one modified, added or omitted a word or a phrase, another would correct him. In this way, it was hoped, nothing could be changed, modified, added or omitted. Texts handed down through an unbroken oral tradition of this kind were considered more reliable and authentic than any record of the teachings set down by a single individual alone many years after the death of their promulgator. The teachings of the Buddha were committed to writing for the first time at a Council in the first century B.C.—held in Ceylon four centuries after his death. Up to that time, the whole of the *Tipiṭaka* had been handed down from generation to generation in this unbroken oral tradition.

The original texts are in Pali, a language soft, melodious and smooth-flowing. Their frequent repetitions, the use of categories, not only help memorization, which is necessary for the continuity of oral tradition, but also give them poetic beauty and charm. They use poetic rhythms and have all the grace of poetry. The recitation of these texts in the original Pali in the calm atmosphere of a tropical grove or in a monastery still produces beautiful, harmonious and serene effects. The sonorous Pali words, their grandeur, and the well-known cadence of repetitions, produce the effect, even for someone who does not know their meaning, of a solemn chant in an unknown tongue. Recitation of this kind with its conventional melodic line, was so peaceful and moving that some narratives related that the deities in the woods were sometimes fascinated and attracted by it.

In the following selections from the original Canon the repetitions are rendered in full only in some places in order to give the reader an idea of their style. In other places they are indicated by dots. I have tried to render the original Pali as closely as possible into English without offending either the sense and tone of the Buddha's words or modern English usage.

SETTING IN MOTION THE WHEEL OF TRUTH
(*Dhammacakkappavattana-sutta*)
(The First Sermon of the Buddha)

Thus have I heard. The Blessed One was once living in the Deer Park at Isipatana (the Resort of Seers) near Bārānasi (Benares). There he addressed the group of five bhikkhus:

'Bhikkhus, these two extremes ought not to be practised by one who has gone forth from the household life. What are the two? There is devotion to the indulgence of sense-pleasures, which is low, common, the way of ordinary people, unworthy and unprofitable; and there is devotion to self-mortification, which is painful, unworthy and unprofitable.

'Avoiding both these extremes, the Tathāgata has realized the Middle Path: it gives vision, it gives knowledge, and it leads to calm, to insight, to enlightenment, to Nibbāna. And what is that

Middle Path . . . ? It is simply the Noble Eightfold Path, namely, right view, right thought, right speech, right action, right livelihood, right effort, right mindfulness, right concentration. This is the Middle Path realized by the Tathāgata, which gives vision, which gives knowledge, and which leads to calm, to insight, to enlightenment, to Nibbāna.

'The Noble Truth of suffering (*Dukkha*) is this: Birth is suffering; aging is suffering; sickness is suffering; death is suffering; sorrow and lamentation, pain, grief and despair are suffering; association with the unpleasant is suffering; dissociation from the pleasant is suffering; not to get what one wants is suffering—in brief, the five aggregates of attachment are suffering.

'The Noble Truth of the origin of suffering is this: It is this thirst (craving) which produces re-existence and re-becoming, bound up with passionate greed. It finds fresh delight now here and now there, namely, thirst for sense-pleasures; thirst for existence and becoming; and thirst for non-existence (self-annihilation).

'The Noble Truth of the Cessation of suffering is this: It is the complete cessation of that very thirst, giving it up, renouncing it, emancipating oneself from it, detaching oneself from it.

'The Noble Truth of the Path leading to the Cessation of suffering is this: It is simply the Noble Eightfold Path, namely right view; right thought; right speech, right action; right livelihood; right effort; right mindfulness; right concentration.

' "This is the Noble Truth of Suffering (Dukkha)": such was the vision, the knowledge, the wisdom, the science, the light, that arose in me with regard to things not heard before. "This suffering, as a noble truth, should be fully understood": such was the vision, the knowledge, the wisdom, the science, the light, that arose in me with regard to things not heard before. "This suffering, as a noble truth, has been fully understood": such was the vision, the knowledge, the wisdom, the science, the light, that arose in me with regard to things not heard before.

' "This is the Noble Truth of the Origin of suffering": such was the vision . . . "This Origin of suffering, as a noble truth, should be abandoned" : such was the vision, . . . "This Origin of suffering, as a noble truth, has been abandoned": such was the vision, . . . with regard to things not heard before.

93

"This is the Noble Truth of the Cessation of suffering": such was the vision . . . "This Cessation of suffering, as a noble truth, should be realized": such was the vision, . . . "This Cessation of suffering, as a noble truth, has been realized": such was the vision, . . . with regard to things not heard before.

' "This is the Noble Truth of the Path leading to the Cessation of suffering": such was the vision, . . . "This Path leading to the Cessation of suffering, as a noble truth, should be followed (cultivated)": such was the vision, . . . "This Path leading to the Cessation of suffering, as a noble truth, has been followed (cultivated)": such was the vision, the knowledge, the wisdom, the science, the light, that arose in me with regard to things not heard before.

'As long as my vision of true knowledge was not fully clear in these three aspects, in these twelve ways, regarding the Four Noble Truths,[1] I did not claim to have realized the perfect Enlightenment that is supreme in the world with its gods, with its Māras and Brahmas, in this world with its recluses and brāhmaṇas, with its princes and men. But when my vision of true knowledge was fully clear in these three aspects, in these twelve ways, regarding the Four Noble Truths, then I claimed to have realized the perfect Enlightenment that is supreme in the world with its gods, its Māras and Brahmas, in this world with its recluses and brāhmaṇas, with its princes and men. And a vision of true knowledge arose in me thus: My heart's deliverance is unassailable. This is the last birth. Now there is no more re-becoming (rebirth).

This the Blessed One said. The group of five bhikkhus was glad, and they rejoiced at his words.

(*Saṃyutta-nikāya*, LVI, 11)

---

[1] As may be seen from the four preceding paragraphs, with regard to each of the Four Noble Truths there are three aspects of knowledge: 1. The knowledge that it is the Truth (*sacca-ñāṇa*) 2. The knowledge that a certain function or action with regard to this Truth should be performed (*kicca-ñāṇa*), and 3. The knowledge that that function or action with regard to this Truth has been performed (*kata-ñāṇa*). When these three aspects are applied to each of the Four Noble Truths, twelve ways are obtained.

THE FIRE SERMON[1]

(*Ādittapariyāya-sutta*)

Thus have I heard. The Blessed One was once living at Gayāsīsa in Gayā with a thousand bhikkhus. There he addressed the bhikkhus:

'Bhikkhus, all is burning. And what is the all that is burning? 'Bhikkhus, the eye is burning, visible forms are burning, visual consciousness is burning, visual impression is burning, also whatever sensation, pleasant or painful or neither-painful-nor-pleasant, arises on account of the visual impression, that too is burning. Burning with what? Burning with the fire of lust, with the fire of hate, with the fire of delusion; I say it is burning with birth, aging and death, with sorrows, with lamentations, with pains, with griefs, with despairs.

'The ear is burning, sounds are burning, auditory consciousness is burning, auditory impression is burning, also whatever sensation, pleasant or painful or neither-painful-nor-pleasant, arises on account of the auditory impression, that too is burning. Burning with what? Burning with the fire of lust. . . . .

'The nose is burning, odours are burning, olfactory consciousness is burning, olfactory impression is burning, also whatever sensation, pleasant or painful or neither-painful-nor-pleasant, arises on account of the olfactory impression, that too is burning. Burning with what? Burning with the fire of lust. . . .

'The tongue is burning, flavours are burning, gustative

[1]It is interesting to note here that Section III of *The Waste Land* by T. S. Eliot is called *The Fire Sermon*. In the note to line 308: 'Burning burning burning burning', Eliot writes: 'The complete text of the Buddha's Fire Sermon (which corresponds in importance to the Sermon on the Mount) from which these words are taken, will be found translated in the late Henry Clarke Warren's *Buddhism in Translation* (Harvard Oriental Series). Mr. Warren was one of the great pioneers of Buddhist studies in the Occident.'

The translation of the *Sutta* given here, made by the present author specially for this edition, is from the original Pali of the *Saṃyutta-nikāya* of the *Sutta-piṭaka*. Warren's translation was of the narrative as found in the *Mahāvagga* of the *Vinaya-piṭaka*.

consciousness is burning, gustative impression is burning, also whatever sensation, pleasant or painful or neither-painful-nor-pleasant, arises on account of the gustative impression, that too is burning. Burning with what? Burning with the fire of lust. . . .

'The body is burning, tangible things are burning, tactile consciousness is burning, tactile impression is burning, also whatever sensation, pleasant or painful or neither-painful-nor-pleasant, arises on account of the tactile sensation, that too is burning. Burning with what? Burning with the fire of lust. . . .

'The mind is burning, mental objects (ideas, etc.) are burning, mental consciousness is burning, mental impression is burning, also whatever sensation, pleasant or painful or neither-painful-nor-pleasant, arises on account of the mental impression, that too is burning. Burning with what? Burning with the fire of lust, with the fire of hate, with the fire of delusion; I say it is burning with birth, aging and death, with sorrows, with lamentations, with pains, with griefs, with despairs.

'Bhikkhus, a learned and noble disciple, who sees (things) thus, becomes dispassionate with regard to the eye, becomes dispassionate with regard to visible forms, becomes dispassionate with regard to the visual consciousness, becomes dispassionate with regard to the visual impression, also whatever sensation, pleasant or painful or neither-painful-nor-pleasant, arises on account of the visual impression, with regard to that too he becomes dispassionate. He becomes dispassionate with regard to the ear, with regard to sounds . . . He becomes dispassionate with regard to the nose . . . with regard to odours . . . He becomes dispassionate with regard to the tongue . . . with regard to flavours . . . He becomes dispassionate with regard to the body . . . with regard to tangible things . . . He becomes dispassionate with regard to the mind, becomes dispassionate with regard to mental objects (ideas, etc.), becomes dispassionate with regard to mental consciousness, becomes dispassionate with regard to mental impression, also whatever sensation, pleasant or painful or neither-painful-nor-pleasant, arises on account of mental impression, with regard to that too he becomes dispassionate.

'Being dispassionate, he becomes detached; through detachment he is liberated. When liberated there is knowledge that he is liberated. And he knows: Birth is exhausted, the holy life has been lived, what has to be done is done, there is no more left to be done on this account.'

This the Blessed One said. The bhikkhus were glad, and they rejoiced at his words.

While this exposition was being delivered, the minds of those thousand bhikkhus were liberated from impurities, without attachment.

(Saṃyutta-nikāya, XXXV, 28)

UNIVERSAL LOVE
(Metta-sutta)

He who is skilled in good and who wishes to attain that state of Calm should act (thus):

He should be able, upright, perfectly upright, compliant, gentle, and humble.

Contented, easily supported, with few duties, of simple livelihood, controlled in senses, discreet, not impudent, he should not be greedily attached to families.

He should not commit any slight wrong such that other wise men might censure him. (Then he should cultivate his thoughts thus:)

May all beings be happy and secure; may their minds be contented.

Whatever living beings there may be—feeble or strong, long (or tall), stout, or medium, short, small, or large, seen or unseen, those dwelling far or near, those who are born and those who are yet to be born—may all beings, without exception, be happy-minded!

Let not one deceive another nor despise any person whatever in any place. In anger or illwill let not one wish any harm to another.

Just as a mother would protect her only child even at the risk of her own life, even so let one cultivate a boundless heart towards all beings.

Let one's thoughts of boundless love pervade the whole world —above, below and across—without any obstruction, without any hatred, without any enmity.

Whether one stands, walks, sits or lies down, as long as one is awake, one should maintain this mindfulness. This, they say, is the Sublime State in this life.

Not falling into wrong views, virtuous and endowed with Insight, one gives up attachment to sense-desires. Verily such a man does not return to enter a womb again.

(Suttanipāta, I. 8)

BLESSINGS
(Maṅgala-sutta)

Thus have I heard:

The Blessed One was once living at the monastery of Anātha-piṇḍika in Jeta's grove, near Sāvatthi. Now when the night was far advanced, a certain deity, whose surpassing splendour illuminated the entire Jeta Grove, came into the presence of the Blessed One, and, drawing near, respectfully saluted Him and stood on one side. Standing thus, he addressed the Blessed One in verse:

'Many deities and men, yearning after happiness, have pondered on Blessings. Pray, tell me the Highest Blessing!'

Not to associate with fools, to associate with the wise, and to honour those who are worthy of honour—this is the Highest Blessing.

To reside in a suitable locality, to have done meritorious actions in the past, and to set oneself in the right course—this is the Highest Blessing.

Vast learning (skill in) handicraft, a highly trained discipline, and pleasant speech—this is the Highest Blessing.

Supporting one's father and mother, cherishing wife and children, and peaceful occupations—this is the Highest Blessing.

Liberality, righteous conduct, the helping of relatives, and blameless actions—this is the Highest Blessing.

To cease and abstain from evil, abstention from intoxicating drinks, and diligence in virtue—this is the Highest Blessing.

Reverence, humility, contentment, gratitude and the opportune hearing of the Dhamma—this is the Highest Blessing.

Patience, obedience, seeing the Samanas (holy men), and (taking part in) religious discussions at proper times—this is the Highest Blessing.

Self-control, Holy Life, perception of the Noble Truths, and the realisation of Nibbāna—this is the Highest Blessing.

If a man's mind is sorrowless, stainless, and secure, and does not shake when touched by worldly vicissitudes—this is the Highest Blessing.

Those who thus acting are everywhere unconquered, attain happiness everywhere—to them these are the Highest Blessings.

(*Suttanipāta*, II. 4)

GETTING RID OF ALL CARES AND TROUBLES

(*Sabbāsava-sutta*)

Thus have I heard. The Blessed One was once living at the monastery of Anāthapiṇḍika in Jeta's grove near Sāvatthi. There he addressed the bhikkhus saying: 'Bhikkhus', and they replied to him: 'Venerable Sir.' The Blessed One spoke as follows:

'Bhikkhus, I will expound to you the method of restraining all cares and troubles.[1] Listen and reflect well; I shall speak to you'. 'Yes, Venerable Sir,' they said in response to the Blessed One.

He then spoke as follows:

'Bhikkhus, I say that the destruction (getting rid) of cares and troubles is (possible) for one who knows and who sees, not for one who does not know and does not see. What must a person know and see in order that the destruction (getting rid) of cares and troubles should be possible? (These are) wise reflection and unwise reflection. For a person who reflects unwisely there arise cares and troubles which have not yet arisen, and (in addition), those which have already arisen increase. But for him who

---

[1]The term *āsava* in this *Sutta* has wider senses than its usual psychological and ethical meanings such as 'influx', 'outflow', 'defilement', 'impurity'. It is here used figuratively and embraces both psychological cares and physical troubles and difficulties as can be seen in the sequel.

reflects wisely, cares and troubles which have not yet arisen do not arise, and (in addition), those already arisen disappear.

'Bhikkhus, (1) there are cares and troubles which are to be got rid of by insight; (2) there are cares and troubles which are to be got rid of by restraint; (3) there are cares and troubles which are to be got rid of by use; (4) there are cares and troubles which are to be got rid of by endurance; (5) there are cares and troubles which are to be got rid of by avoidance; (6) there are cares and troubles which are to be got rid of by dispersal; (7) there are cares and troubles which are to be got rid of by culture.

(1) 'Bhikkhus, what are the cares and troubles which are to be got rid of by insight? Bhikkhus, the uninstructed ordinary man, who does not see the Noble Ones, who is unversed in the Teachings of the Noble Ones, who is untrained in the Teachings of the Noble Ones, who does not see good men, who is unversed in the Teachings of good men, who is untrained in the Teachings of good men, does not understand what things should be reflected on and what things should not be reflected on. Not knowing what things should be reflected on and what things should not be reflected on, he reflects on things that should not be reflected on, and does not reflect on things that should be reflected on.

'Now, Bhikkhus, what are the things that should not be reflected on but on which he reflects? If, in a person, reflecting on certain things, there arises the defilement of sense-pleasure which has not yet arisen, and (in addition), the defilement of sense-pleasure which has already arisen in him increases, the defilement of (the desire for) existence and for becoming . . . the defilement of ignorance which has not yet arisen arises and (in addition), the defilement of ignorance which has already arisen in him increases, then these are the things that should not be reflected on, but on which he reflects.

Bhikkhus, what are the things that should be reflected on, but on which he does not reflect? If, in a person, reflecting on certain things, the defilement of sense-pleasure which has not yet arisen does not arise, and (in addition), the defilement of sense-pleasure which has already arisen in him disappears, the defilement of (the desire for) existence and for becoming . . . the defilement of ignorance which has not yet arisen does not arise, and (in addition), the defilement of ignorance which has already arisen in him disappears, these are the things that should be reflected on, but on which he does not reflect.

'By reflecting on things that should not be reflected on, and by not reflecting on things that should be reflected on, defilements that have not yet arisen arise, and defilements that have already arisen in him increase. Then he reflects unwisely (unnecessarily) in this way:

1. Did I exist in the past?
2. Did I not exist in the past?
3. What was I in the past?
4. How was I in the past?
5. Having been what, did I become what in the past?
6. Shall I exist in future?
7. Shall I not exist in future?
8. What shall I be in future?
9. How shall I be in future?
10. Having been what, shall I become what in future?

Or, now at the present time he is doubtful about himself:

11. Am I?
12. Am I not?
13. What am I?
14. How am I?
15. Whence came this person?
16. Whither will he go?

When he reflects unwisely in this way, one of the six false views arises in him:

1. I have a Self: this view arises in him as true and real.
2. I have no Self: this view arises in him as true and real.
3. By Self I perceive Self: this view arises in him as true and real.
4. By Self I perceive non-self: this view arises in him as true and real.
5. By non-self I perceive Self: this view arises in him as true and real.
6. Or a wrong view arises in him as follows: This my Self, which speaks and feels, which experiences the fruits of good and bad actions now here and now there, this Self is permanent, stable, everlasting, unchanging, remaining the same for ever and ever.

'This, Bhikkhus, is what is called becoming enmeshed in views; a jungle of views, a wilderness of views; scuffling in views, the agitation (struggle) of views, the fetter of views. Bhikkhus, the uninstructed ordinary man fettered by the fetters of views, does not liberate himself from birth, aging and death, from sorrows, lamentations, pains, griefs, despairs; I say that he does not liberate himself from suffering (*dukkha*).

'And, Bhikkhus, the instructed noble disciple, who sees the Noble Ones, who is versed in the Teachings of the Noble Ones, who is well trained in the Teachings of the Noble Ones, who sees good men, who is versed in the Teachings of the good men, who is well trained in the teachings of the good men, knows what things should be reflected on and what should not be reflected on. Knowing what things should be reflected on and what should not be reflected on, he does not reflect on things that should not be reflected on and he reflects on things that should be reflected on.

'Now, Bhikkhus, what are the things that should not be reflected on which he does not reflect? If, in a person, reflecting on certain things, there arises the defilement of sense-pleasure which has not yet arisen, and (in addition), the defilement of sense-pleasure which has already arisen in him increases, the defilement of (the desire for) existence and for becoming . . . the defilement of ignorance which has not yet arisen arises, and the defilement of ignorance which has already arisen in him increases, these are the things that should not be reflected on, and on which he does not reflect.

'Bhikkhus, what are the things that should be reflected on, and on which he reflects? If, in a person, reflecting on certain things, the defilement of sense-pleasure which has not yet arisen does not arise, and (in addition), the defilement of sense-pleasure which has already arisen in him disappears, the defilement of (the desire for) existence and for becoming . . . the defilement of ignorance which has not yet arisen does not arise, and (in addition), the defilement of ignorance which has already arisen in him disappears, these are the things that should be reflected on, and on which he reflects.

By not reflecting on things that should not be reflected on, and by reflecting on things that should be reflected on, the defilements that have not yet arisen do not arise, and (in addition), the defilements that have already arisen in him disappear. Then he reflects wisely: This is *Dukkha* (suffering). He reflects wisely: This is the arising (cause) of *Dukkha*. He reflects wisely: This is the Cessation of *Dukkha*. He reflects wisely: This is the Path leading to the Cessation of *Dukkha*. When he reflects wisely in this manner, the three Fetters—the false idea of self, sceptical doubt, attachment to observances and rites—fall away from him. Bhikkhus, these are called the troubles (defilements, fetters) that should be got rid of by insight.

(2) 'Bhikkhus, what are the cares and troubles to be got rid of by restraint?

'Bhikkhus, a bhikkhu, considering wisely, lives with his eyes restrained. Now, if there are any troubles, distresses and vexations for him when he lives without restraining his eyes, those troubles, distresses and vexations are not for him when he lives restraining his eyes in this manner.

'Considering wisely, he lives with his ears restrained . . . with his nose restrained . . . with his tongue . . . with his body . . . with his mind restrained. Now, if there are any troubles, distresses and vexations for him when he lives without restraining his mind, those troubles, distresses and vexations are not for him when he lives restraining his mind in this manner. Bhikkhus, these are called the cares and troubles to be got rid of by restraint.

(3) 'Bhikkhus, what are the cares and troubles to be got rid of by use? Bhikkhus, a bhikkhu, considering wisely, makes use of his robes—only to keep off cold, to keep off heat, to keep off gadflies, mosquitoes, winds and the sun, and creeping creatures, and to cover himself decently. Considering wisely, he makes use of food—neither for pleasures nor for excess (intoxication), neither for beauty nor for adornment, but only to support and sustain this body, to keep it from hurt (fatigue) and to foster the holy life, thinking: In this way I put out the feeling (of suffering, hunger) which is already there, and will not produce a new feeling, and my life will be maintained in blamelessness (harmlessness) and convenience. Considering wisely, he makes use of lodging—only to keep off cold, to keep off heat, to keep off gadflies, mosquitoes, winds and the sun, and creeping creatures, to dispel the risks of the seasons and to enjoy seclusion. Consider-

ing wisely, he makes use of medicaments and medical requirements—only to get rid of pains and illnesses which he may have and to maintain his health. Bhikkhus, if there are any troubles, distresses and vexations for him who does not use any (of these things), these troubles, distresses and vexations are not for him when he uses (them) in this manner. Bhikkhus, these are called the cares and troubles which are to be got rid of by use.

(4) 'Bhikkhus, what are the cares and troubles to be got rid of by endurance? Bhikkhus, a bhikkhu, considering wisely, puts up with cold and heat, hunger and thirst, with gadflies, mosquitoes, winds, the sun and creeping creatures, abusive and hurtful language, he becomes inured to endurance of bodily feelings which are painful, acute, sharp, severe, unpleasant, disagreeable, deadly. Bhikkhus, if there are any troubles, distresses and vexations for a person who does not endure any (of these), those troubles, distresses and vexations are not for him who endures them in this manner. Bhikkhus, these are called the cares and troubles which are to be got rid of by endurance.

(5) 'Bhikkhus, what are the cares and troubles to be got rid of by avoidance? Bhikkhus, a bhikkhu, considering wisely, avoids a savage elephant, a savage horse, a savage bull, a savage dog, avoids a snake, the stump (of a tree), a thorny hedge, a pit (hole), a precipice, a refuse-pool or a dirty pool. Considering wisely, he also avoids sitting in such unseemly places, and frequenting such unseemly resorts, and cultivating such bad friends as would lead the discreet among his fellows in the holy life to conclude that he has gone astray. Bhikkhus, if there are any troubles, distresses and vexations for him when he does not avoid any things (such as these), those troubles, distresses and vexations would not be for him when he avoids them in this manner. These are called the cares and troubles which are to be got rid of by avoidance.

(6) 'What are the cares and troubles to be got rid of by dispersal? Bhikkhus, a bhikkhu, considering wisely, does not tolerate, rejects, discards, destroys, extinguishes thoughts of sense-pleasure which have arisen in him; he does not tolerate . . . thoughts of ill-will . . . he does not tolerate . . . thoughts of violence . . . he does not tolerate, rejects, discards, destroys, extinguishes whatever evil and unwholesome thoughts which

have arisen in him. Bhikkhus, if there are any troubles, distresses, and vexations for him when he does not disperse any (of these), those troubles, distresses and vexations would not be for him when he disperses them in this manner. Bhikkhus, these are called the cares and troubles which are to be got rid of by dispersal.

(7) 'Bhikkhus, what are the cares and troubles to be got rid of by culture (*bhāvanā*)? Bhikkhus, a bhikkhu, considering wisely, cultivates mindfulness, a Factor of Enlightenment associated with detachment, with passionlessness, with cessation, maturing into renunciation; considering wisely, he cultivates the Investigation of the Dhamma, a Factor of Enlightenment . . . Energy, a Factor of Enlightenment . . . Joy, a Factor of Enlightenment . . . Calmness (Relaxation), a Factor of Enlightenment . . . Concentration, a Factor of Enlightenment . . . Equanimity, a Factor of Enlightenment associated with detachment, with passionlessness, with cessation, maturing into renunciation. Bhikkhus, if there are any troubles, distresses and vexations for him when he does not cultivate any (of these), those troubles, distresses and vexations would not be for him when he cultivates them in this manner. Bhikkhus, these are called the cares and troubles which are to be got rid of by culture.

'Bhikkhus, a bhikkhu in whom the cares and troubles which are to be got rid of by insight have been got rid of by insight; the cares and troubles which are to be got rid of by restraint have been got rid of by restraint; the cares and troubles which are to be got rid of by use have been got rid of by use; the cares and troubles which are to be got rid of by endurance have been got rid of by endurance; the cares and troubles which are to be got rid of by avoidance have been got rid of by avoidance; the cares and troubles which are to be got rid of by dispersal have been got rid of by dispersal; the cares and troubles which are to be got rid of by culture have been got rid of by culture— Bhikkhus, it is this bhikkhu who is said to have restrained all cares and troubles; he has cut off craving, struck off his fetters, and by fathoming false pride, has put an end to suffering.'

Thus spoke the Blessed One. Glad at heart, those bhikkhus rejoiced at the words of the Blessed One.

(*Majjhima-nikāya,* No. 2)

THE PARABLE OF THE PIECE OF CLOTH
(*Vatthūpama-sutta*)
(Abridged)

Thus have I heard. The Blessed One was once living at the monastery of Anāthapiṇḍika in Jeta's grove near Sāvatthi. There the Blessed One addressed the bhikkhus saying: 'Bhikkhus' and they replied to him: 'Venerable Sir'. The Blessed One then spoke as follows:
    'If a soiled and dirty (piece of) cloth is dipped by the fuller in any dye at all—blue, yellow, red or pink—it will still be of bad and dirty colour. Why? Because the cloth is not clean. Even so, Bhikkhus, when the mind is impure, a bad future life must be expected.
    'If a perfectly clean (piece of) cloth is dipped by the fuller in any dye at all—blue, yellow, red or pink—it will be of beautiful and clean colour. Why? Because the cloth is clean. Even so, Bhikkhus, when the mind is pure, a good future life must be expected.
    'Now, what are the mind's impurities? Cupidity—excessive desire—is an impurity of the mind; enmity . . . anger . . . rancour . . . hypocrisy . . . malice . . . jealousy . . . avarice . . . trickery . . . deceit . . . obduracy . . . haughtiness . . . pride . . . arrogance . . . inflation . . . indolence is an impurity of the mind.
    'Bhikkhus, that bhikkhu, who recognizes cupidity—excessive desire—as an impurity of the mind, abandons it; who recognizes enmity . . . anger . . . rancour . . . hypocrisy . . . malice . . . jealousy . . . avarice . . . trickery . . . deceit . . . obduracy . . . haughtiness . . . pride . . . arrogance . . . inflation . . . indolence as an impurity of the mind, abandons it.
    'Bhikkhus, when that bhikkhu has abandoned cupidity—excessive desire—recognizing it as an impurity of the mind; when he has abandoned enmity . . . anger . . . rancour . . . hypocrisy . . . malice . . . jealousy . . . avarice . . . trickery . . . deceit . . . obduracy . . . haughtiness . . . pride . . . arrogance . . . inflation . . . indolence recognizing it as an impurity of the mind, he finds serene joy (satisfaction) in the Enlightened One: (knowing that)

"The Blessed One is Worthy, Perfectly Enlightened, Endowed with knowledge and virtue, Happy, Knower of worlds, Matchless tamer of men, Teacher of gods and men, Awakened and Blessed." He finds serene joy (satisfaction) in the Dhamma: (knowing that) "The Dhamma is excellently expounded by the Blessed One; it can be realized here in this life; it produces immediate results; it invites people to come and see (investigate); it leads to the goal (Nibbāna); it has to be comprehended by the wise, each for himself." He finds serene joy (satisfaction) in the Community of the Disciples: (knowing that) "The Community of the Disciples of the Blessed One is of good conduct, upright, wise, dutiful. The Community of the Disciples of the Blessed One: namely, the Four Pairs of Persons, the Eight kinds of Individuals,[1] is worthy of offerings, of hospitality, of gifts, of reverential salutation, it is an incomparable field of merit to the world."

'Finally, with impurities renounced, spewed out, discharged, abandoned, and with the thought that he is endowed with serene joy in the Enlightened One—in his Teaching (*Dhamma*)—in the Community—he is touched with a feeling for the Sense and the Truth, and he receives the gladness associated with Truth; when one is glad, joy arises; when the mind is joyful, the body becomes relaxed; when relaxed, one feels content: the mind of the contented man is concentrated.

'A bhikkhu who has reached this state in virtue, in mental discipline and in wisdom, may, without impediment (to his spiritual life), partake of the choicest rice with all manner of sauces and curries. Just as a soiled and dirty cloth, plunged in clear water, becomes pure and clean; or just as gold, passed through the furnace, becomes pure and clean; even so, a bhikkhu who has reached this state in virtue, in mental discipline and in wisdom, may partake of the choicest rice with all manner of sauces and curries, and it will not be an impediment (harm) to him (to his spiritual life).

[1]The Four Pairs of Persons constitute the four kinds of disciples who have attained the four Paths and the four Fruits of Sainthood, namely, *Sotāpatti* (Stream-Entrant), *Sakadāgāmi* (Once-Returner), *Anāgāmi* (Never-Returner), and *Arahatta* (Worthy). The one who has attained the Path and the one who has attained the Fruit of each of the four stages of Sainthood are once taken together and considered as a Pair. Hence the Four Pairs of Persons. And then when the two persons of each Pair are regarded separately, there are eight Individuals.

'With thoughts of love—of compassion—of sympathetic joy—of equanimity—he pervades one quarter of the world, so too the second, the third and the fourth quarters, above, below, across, everywhere; the whole length and breadth of the wide world is pervaded by the radiant thoughts of a mind all-embracing, vast and boundless, without hate, without ill-will.

'Then he knows: "There is this; there is a lower and there is yet a higher stage; Deliverance lies beyond this realm of perceptions." When he knows and sees this, his mind becomes liberated from the impurities of sense-pleasure, of (the desire for) continuing existence, of ignorance. When liberated, there is knowledge that he is liberated. Then he knows: "Birth is exhausted, the holy life has been lived, what has to be done is done, there is no more left to be done on this account." Bhikkhus, such a bhikkhu can be said to have bathed internally.'

Now at this time there was sitting close by the Brahmin Sundarika-Bhāradvāja who asked the Blessed One thus: 'Does the Venerable Gotama go to bathe in the river Bāhukā?'

'What does the river Bāhukā matter, Brahmin? What (good) does it do?'

'Venerable Gotama, the river Bāhukā is considered by many people as purifying, as holy. Many people wash away their sins in the river Bāhukā.'

Thereupon the Blessed One addressed the Brahmin Sundarika-Bhāradvāja in these lines:

'In Bāhukā and in Adhikakkā,
Gayā, Sundarikā, Srassatī,
Payāga, Bāhumatī—there the fool of black deeds
May daily plunge, yet is never purified.
What can Sundarikā, Payāga or Bāhumatī do?
They cleanse not the man guilty of hate and evil.
For him who is pure (in mind) any day is auspicious, any day is hallowed.
Cleansed, pure in deeds,
He always fulfils observances.
So, Brahmin, come and bathe here.
Love all that lives. If you neither lie, nor slay, nor steal,
Are no greedy miser but live in trust,
What use going to Gayā? Your well at home is Gayā.'

At this the Brahmin Sundarika-Bhāradvāja said to the Blessed One: 'Excellent, Venerable Gotama, excellent! It is just as if one should set upright what had been turned upside down, or reveal what had been hidden away, or show the way to a man gone astray, or bring a lamp into darkness so that those with eyes might see things there. In this manner in many ways the Dhamma is expounded by the Venerable Gotama. I take refuge in the Venerable Gotama, in the Dhamma and in the Community of Bhikkhus. May I be admitted into the Order and receive the Higher Ordination under the Venerable Gotama.'

The Brahmin Sundarika-Bhāradvāja was admitted into the Order and received the Higher Ordination. Not long after his Higher Ordination, the Venerable Bhāradvāja, dwelling alone and aloof, strenuous, ardent, resolute, attained to and dwelt in that incomparable State, the ultimate aim of holy life, in quest of which sons of families go forth from home to homelessness. And he knew through higher knowledge: 'Birth is exhausted, the holy life has been lived, what has to be done is done, there is no more left to be done on this account.' And in this way the Venerable Bhāradvāja, too, became one of the Arahants.

(*Majjhima-nikāya*, Sutta No. 7)

THE FOUNDATIONS OF MINDFULNESS
(The Presence of Mindfulness)
(*Satipaṭṭhāna-sutta*)
(Abridged)

Thus have I heard. The Blessed One was once living among the Kurus, at Kammāssadamma, a market town of the Kuru people. There the Blessed One addressed the bhikkhus and spoke as follows:

'This is the only way, Bhikkhus, for the purification of beings, for the overcoming of sorrow and lamentation, for the destruction of suffering and grief, for reaching the right path, for the attainment of Nibbāna, namely the Four Foundations (four forms of Presence) of Mindfulness. What are the four?

'Here a bhikkhu, ardent, clearly comprehending things and

mindful, lives observing (the activities of) the body, having overcome covetousness and repugnance towards the world (of body); observing feelings, having overcome covetousness and repugnance towards the world (of feelings)... observing (the activities of) the mind, having overcome covetousness and repugnance towards the world (of mind); observing mental objects, having overcome covetousness and repugnance towards the world (of mental objects).'

(I. BODY)

'And how does a bhikkhu live observing (the activities of) the body?

[1. *Breathing*]

'Here Bhikkhus, a bhikkhu having gone to the forest, to the foot of a tree or to some empty place, sits down, with his legs crossed, keeps his body straight and his mindfulness alert.

'Ever mindful he breathes in, and ever mindful he breathes out. Breathing in a long breath, he knows "I am breathing in a long breath"; breathing out a long breath, he knows "I am breathing out a long breath"; breathing in a short breath, he knows "I am breathing in a short breath"; breathing out a short breath, he knows "I am breathing out a short breath".

' "Experiencing the whole (breath-) body, I shall breathe in"; thus he trains himself. "Experiencing the whole (breath-) body, I shall breathe out": thus he trains himself. "Calming the activity of the (breath-) body, I shall breath in": thus he trains himself. "Calming the activity of the (breath-) body, I shall breathe out": thus he trains himself. ...

'Thus he lives observing (the activities of) the body internally, or ... externally, or ... both internally and externally. He lives also observing origination-factors in the body, or dissolution-factors in the body, or origination-and-dissolution factors in the body. Or his mindfulness is established to the extent necessary just for knowledge and awareness that the body exists and he lives unattached, and clings to naught in the world. In this way Bhikkhus, a bhikkhu lives observing (the activities of) the body.

[2. *Postures of the body*]

'And further, Bhikkhus, a bhikkhu knows when he is going, "I am going". He knows when he is standing, "I am standing".

He knows when he is sitting, "I am sitting". He knows when he is lying down, "I am lying down". Or he knows just how his body is disposed.

'Thus he lives observing (the activities of) the body internally, or externally . . .

[3. *Full Attention*]

'And further, Bhikkhus, a bhikkhu applies full attention either in going forward or back; in looking straight on or looking away; in bending or in stretching; in wearing robes or carrying the bowl; in eating, drinking, chewing or savouring; in attending to the calls of nature; in walking, in standing, in sitting; in falling asleep, in waking; in speaking or in keeping silence. In all these he applies full attention.

'Thus he lives observing (the activities of) the body.

[4. *Repulsiveness of the body*]

'And further, Bhikkhus, a bhikkhu reflects on this very body enveloped by the skin and full of manifold impurity, from the sole up, and from the top of the hair down, thinking thus: "There are in this body hair of the head, hair of the body, nails, teeth, skin, flesh, sinews, bones, marrow, kidneys, heart, liver, midriff, spleen, lungs, intestines, mesentery, stomach, fasces, bile, phlegm, pus, blood, sweat, fat, tears, grease, saliva, nasal mucus, synovial fluid, urine".

'Just as if there were a double-mouthed provision-bag full of various kinds of grain such as hill paddy, paddy, green gram, cow-peas, sesamum and husked rice, and a man with sound eyes, having opened that bag, were to reflect thus: This is hill paddy, this is paddy, this is green gram, this is cow-pea, this is sesamum, this is husked rice, just so, Bhikkhus, a bhikkhu reflects on this very body enveloped by the skin and full of manifold impurity, from the sole up, and from the top of the hair down, thinking thus: There are in this body hair of the head, hair of the body, nails, teeth . . . synovial fluid, urine.

'Thus he lives observing the body. . . .

[5. *Material Elements*]

'And further, Bhikkhus, a bhikkhu reflects on this very body, as it is, and it is constituted, by way of the material elements: "There are in this body the element of earth, the element of water, the element of fire, the element of wind".

'Just as if, Bhikkhus, a clever cow-butcher or his apprentice, having slaughtered a cow and divided it into portions, would be sitting at the junction of four high roads; in the same way, a bhikkhu reflects on this very body, as it is, and it is constituted, by way of the material elements: "There are in this body the elements of earth, water, fire and wind".

'Thus he lives observing the body. . . .

[6. *Nine Cemetery Objects*]

(1) 'And further, Bhikkhus, just as a bhikkhu sees a body dead one, two, or three days, swollen, blue and festering, thrown on to the cemetery, so he applies this perception to his own body thus: "Verily, my own body, too, is of the same nature; such it will become and will not escape it".

'Thus he lives observing the body. . . .

(2) 'And further, Bhikkhus, just as a bhikkhu sees a body thrown on to the cemetery, being eaten by crows, hawks, vultures, dogs, jackals or by different kinds of worms, so he applies this perception to his own body thus: "Verily, my own body, too, is of the same nature; such it will become and will not escape it".

'Thus he lives observing the body. . . .

(3) 'And further, Bhikkhus, just as a bhikkhu sees a body thrown on to the cemetery reduced to a skeleton with some flesh and blood attached to it, held together by the tendons. . . .

(4) 'And further, Bhikkhus, just as a bhikkhu sees a body thrown on to the cemetery reduced to a skeleton, blood-besmeared and without flesh, held together by the tendons. . . .

(5) 'And further, Bhikkhus, just as a bhikkhu sees a body thrown on to the cemetery reduced to a skeleton without flesh and blood, held together by the tendons. . . .

(6) 'And further, Bhikkhus, just as a bhikkhu sees a body thrown on to the cemetery reduced to disconnected bones, scattered in all directions—here a bone of the hand, there a bone of the foot, a shin bone, a thigh bone, the pelvis, spine and skull. . . .

(7) 'And further, Bhikkhus, just as a bhikkhu sees a body thrown on to the cemetery reduced to bleached bones of conch-like colour. . . .

(8) 'And further, Bhikkhus, just as a bhikkhu sees a body

thrown on to the cemetery reduced to bones, more than a year old, lying in a heap. . . .

(9) 'And further, Bhikkhus, just as a bhikkhu sees a body thrown on to the cemetery reduced to bones rotten and become dust . . . so he applies this perception to his own body thus: "Verily, my own body, too, is of the same nature; such it will become and will not escape it".

'Thus he lives observing the body . . .'

[11. FEELINGS]

'And how Bhikkhus, does a bhikkhu live observing feelings?

'Here, Bhikkhus, a bhikkhu when experiencing a pleasant feeling knows: "I experience a pleasant feeling"; when experiencing a painful feeling, he knows: "I experience a painful feeling"; when experiencing a neither-pleasant-nor-painful feeling, he knows: "I experience a neither-pleasant-nor-painful feeling". When experiencing a pleasant wordly feeling, he knows: "I experience a pleasant worldly feeling"; when experiencing a pleasant spiritual feeling, he knows: "I experience a pleasant spiritual feeling"; when experiencing a painful worldly feeling, he knows: "I experience a painful worldly feeling"; when experiencing a painful spiritual feeling, he knows: "I experience a painful spiritual feeling"; when experiencing a neither-pleasant-nor-painful worldly feeling, he knows: "I experience a neither-pleasant-nor-painful worldly feeling"; when experiencing a neither-pleasant-nor-painful spiritual feeling, he knows: "I experience a neither-pleasant-nor-painful spiritual feeling".

'He lives in this way observing feelings internally, . . . or externally, or . . . internally and externally. He lives observing origination-factors in feelings, or dissolution-factors in feelings, or origination-and-dissolution factors in feelings. Or his mindfulness is established to the extent necessary just for knowledge and awareness that feeling exists, and he lives unattached, and clings to naught in the world. In this way, Bhikkhus, a bhikkhu lives observing feelings.'

[III. MIND]

'And how, Bhikkhus, does a bhikkhu live observing mind?

'Here Bhikkhus, a bhikkhu knows the mind with lust, as being with lust; the mind without lust, as being without lust; the mind with hate, as being with hate; the mind without hate, as being without hate; the mind with ignorance, as being with ignorance; the mind without ignorance, as being without ignorance; the shrunken state of mind as the shrunken state; the distracted state of mind as the distracted state; the developed state of mind as the developed state; the undeveloped state of mind as the undeveloped state; the state of mind with some other mental state superior to it, as being the state with something mentally superior to it; the state of mind with no other mental state superior to it, as being the state with nothing mentally superior to it; the concentrated state of mind as the concentrated state; the unconcentrated state of mind as the unconcentrated state; the liberated state of mind as the liberated state; and the unliberated state of mind as the unliberated state.

'He lives in this way observing the mind internally, or externally, or internally and externally.

He lives observing origination-factors in mind or dissolution-factors in mind or origination-and-dissolution-factors in mind. Or his mindfulness is established to the extent necessary just for knowledge and awareness that mind exists, and he lives unattached, and clings to naught in the world. Thus, Bhikkhus, a bhikkhu lives observing mind.'

[IV. MENTAL OBJECTS]

'And how, Bhikkhus, does a bhikkhu live observing mental objects?

[*Five Hindrances*]

'Here, Bhikkhus, a bhikkhu lives observing the Five Hindrances as mental objects.

'How, Bhikkhus, does a bhikkhu live observing the Five Hindrances as mental objects?

(1) 'Here, Bhikkhus, when sense-desire is present, a bhikkhu knows: "Sense-desire is in me", or when sense-desire is not present, he knows: "There is no sense-desire in me". He knows how the non-arisen sense-desire arises; he knows how the arisen sense-desire disappears; and he knows how the non-arising in the future of the abandoned sense-desire comes to be.

114

(2) 'When anger is present, he knows: "Anger is in me". . . .

(3) 'When torpor and languor are present, he knows: "Torpor and languor are in me". . . .

(4) 'When restlessness and worry are present, he knows: "Restlessness and worry are in me". . . . .

(5) 'When doubt is present, he knows: "Doubt is in me", or when doubt is not present, he knows, "There is no doubt in me". He knows how the non-arisen doubt arises; he knows how the arisen doubt disappears; and he knows how the non-arising in the future of the abandoned doubt comes to be.

'In this way he lives observing mental objects internally, or externally, or internally and externally. He lives observing origination-factors in mental objects, or dissolution-factors in mental objects, or origination- and dissolution-factors in mental objects. Or his mindfulness is established to the extent necessary just for knowledge and awareness that mental objects exist, and he lives unattached and clings to naught in the world. In this way, Bhikkhus, a bhikkhu lives observing the five hindrances as mental objects.

[Five Aggregates]

'And further, Bhikkhus, a bhikkhu lives observing the five aggregates of clinging as mental objects.

'How, Bhikkhus, does a bhikkhu live observing (contemplating) the five aggregates of clinging as mental objects?

'Here, Bhikkhus, a bhikku thinks: Thus is material form; it arises in this way; and it disappears in this way. Thus is feeling; it arises in this way; and it disappears in this way. Thus is perception; it arises in this way; and it disappears in this way. Thus are mental formations; they arise in this way; and they disappear in this way. Thus is consciousness; it arises in this way; and it disappears in this way.

'Thus he lives contemplating mental objects internally, etc. . . . In this way, Bhikkhus, a bhikkhu lives contemplating the five aggregates of clinging as mental objects.

[Six Sense-Bases]

'And further, Bhikkhus, a bhikkhu lives contemplating the six internal and the six external sense-bases as mental objects.

'How, Bhikkhus, does a bhikkhu live contemplating the six internal and the six external sense-bases as mental objects?

'Here, Bhikkhus, a bhikkhu knows the eye and visual forms, and the fetter that arises dependent on both (the eye and forms); he knows how the non-arisen fetter arises; he knows how the arisen fetter disappears; and he knows how the non-arising in the future of the abandoned fetter comes to be.

'He knows the ear and sounds . . . the nose and smells . . . the tongue and flavours . . . the body and tangible objects . . . the mind and mental objects, and the fetter that arises dependent on both; he knows how the non-arisen fetter arises; he knows how the arisen fetter disappears; and he knows how the non-arising in the future of the abandoned fetter comes to be.

'In this way, Bhikkhus, a bhikkhu lives contemplating mental objects internally, etc. . . . In this way, Bhikkhus, a bhikkhu lives contemplating the six internal and the six external sense-bases as mental objects.

[*Seven Factors of Enlightenment*]
'And further, Bhikkhus, a bhikkhu lives observing the Seven Factors of Enlightenment as mental objects.

'How Bhikkhus does a bhikkhu live observing the Seven Factors of Enlightenment as mental objects?

(1) 'Here Bhikkhus, when the Enlightenment-factor of Mindfulness is present, the bhikkhu knows: "The Enlightenment-factor of Mindfulness is in me"; or when the Enlightenment-factor of Mindfulness is absent, he knows: "The Enlightenment-factor of Mindfulness is not in me"; and he knows how the non-arisen Enlightenment-factor of Mindfulness arises; and how perfection in the development of the arisen Enlightenment-factor of Mindfulness comes to be.

(2) 'When the Enlightenment-factor of the Investigation of mental objects is present, the bhikkhu knows: "The Enlightenment-factor of the Investigation of mental objects is in me"; when the Enlightenment-factor of the Investigation of mental objects is absent, he knows: "The Enlightenment-factor of the Investigation of mental objects is not in me"; and he knows how the non-arisen Enlightenment-factor of the Investigation of mental objects arises and how perfection in the development of

116

the arisen Enlightenment-factor of the Investigation of mental objects comes to be.

(3) When the Enlightenment-factor of Energy is present, he knows: "The Enlightenment-factor of Energy is in me"; when the Enlightenment-factor of Energy is absent, he knows: "The Enlightenment-factor of Energy is not in me"; and he knows how the non-arisen Enlightenment-factor of Energy arises, and how perfection in the development of the arisen Enlightenment-factor of Energy comes to be.

(4) 'When the Enlightenment-factor of Joy is present, he knows: "The Enlightenment-factor of Joy is in me"; when the Enlightenment-factor of Joy is absent, he knows: "The Enlightenment-factor of Joy is not in me"; and he knows how the non-arisen Enlightenment-factor of Joy arises and how perfection in the development of the arisen Enlightenment-factor of Joy comes to be.

(5) 'When the Enlightenment-factor of Relaxation (of body and mind) is present, he knows: "The Enlightenment-factor of Relaxation is in me"; when the Enlightenment-factor of Relaxation is absent, he knows: "The Enlightenment-factor of Relaxation is not in me"; and he knows how the non-arisen Enlightenment-factor of Relaxation arises, and how perfection in the development of the arisen Enlightenment-factor of the Relaxation comes to be.

(6) 'When the Enlightenment-factor of Concentration is present, he knows: "The Enlightenment-factor of Concentration is in me"; when the Enlightenment-factor of Concentration is absent, he knows: "The Enlightenment-factor of Concentration is not in me"; and he knows how the non-arisen Enlightenment-factor of Concentration arises, and how perfection in the development of the arisen Enlightenment-factor of Concentration comes to be.

(7) 'When the Enlightenment-factor of Equanimity is present, he knows: "The Enlightenment-factor of Equanimity is in me"; when the Enlightenment-factor of Equanimity is absent, he knows: "The Enlightenment-factor of Equanimity is not in me"; and he knows how the non-arisen Enlightenment-factor of Equanimity arises, and how perfection in the development of the arisen Enlightenment-factor of Equanimity comes to be.

'Thus he lives observing mental objects internally, etc. . . .
Thus, Bhikkhus, a bhikkhu lives observing the Seven Factors of
Enlightenment as mental objects.

[*Four Noble Truths*]
'And further, Bhikkhus, a bhikkhu lives contemplating
the Four Noble Truths as mental objects.
'How Bhikkhus, does a bhikkhu live contemplating the Four
Noble Truths as mental objects?
'Here, Bhikkhus, a bhikkhu knows, "This is *Dukkha* (suffer-
ing)", according to reality; he knows, "This is the Origin of
Dukkha", according to reality; he knows, "This the Cessation of
Dukkha", according to reality; he knows, "This is the Path
leading to the Cessation of *Dukkha*", according to reality.
'Thus he lives contemplating mental objects internally, etc. . . .
In this way, Bhikkhus, a bhikkhu lives contemplating the Four
Noble Truths as mental objects.
'Bhikkhus, whosoever practises these four Foundations of
Mindfulness in this manner for seven years, then one of these
two fruits may be expected by him: Highest Knowledge (Arahant-
ship), here and now, or if some remainder of clinging is yet
present, the state of Non-returning.
'Bhikkhus, let alone seven years. Should any person practise
these four Foundations of Mindfulness in this manner for six
years . . . for five years . . . four years . . . three years . . . two
years . . . one year, then one of these two fruits may be expected
by him: Highest Knowledge, here and now, or if some remainder
of clinging is yet present, the state of Non-returning.
'Bhikkhus, let alone a year. Should any person practise these
four Foundations of Mindfulness in this manner for seven
months . . . for six months . . . five months . . . four months . . .
three months . . . two months . . . a month . . . half a month, then
one of these two fruits may be expected by him: Highest Knowledge, here and now, or if some remainder of clinging is yet
present, the state of Non-returning.
'Bhikkhus, let alone half a month. Should any person practise
these four Foundations of Mindfulness, in this manner, for a
week, then one of these two fruits may be expected by him:
Highest Knowledge, here and now, or if some remainder of

clinging is yet present, the state of Non-returning.
'Because of this was it said: "This is the only way, Bhikkhus, for the purification of beings, for the overcoming of sorrow and lamentation, for the destruction of suffering and grief, for reaching the right path, for the attainment of Nibbāna, namely the four Foundations of Mindfulness".'
This the Blessed One said. Satisfied, the Bhikkhus rejoiced at his words.

(Majjhima Nikāya, Sutta No. 10)

ADVICE TO SIGALA
(Domestic and Social Relations)
(*Sigālovāda-sutta*)
(Abridged)

Thus have I heard. The Blessed One was once staying near Rājagaha at the Squirrels' Feeding-ground in the Bamboo Wood.

Now at this time Sigāla, a householder's son, rising early, went out of Rājagaha. With wet hair, wet garments and his clasped hands uplifted, he performed the rite of worship to the several quarters of earth and sky: to the east, south, west, and north, to the nadir and the zenith.[1]

Early that same morning, the Blessed One dressed, took bowl and robe and entered Rājagaha seeking alms. He saw Sigāla at his rite of worship and spoke to him thus:

'Why, young householder, do you, rising early and leaving Rājagaha, with your hair and raiment wet, worship the several quarters of earth and sky?'

'Sir, my father, when he was on his death-bed, said to me: "Dear son, you should worship the quarters of earth and sky." So I, sir, honouring my father's word, reverencing, revering,

---

[1]Performing the rite of worship of the different quarters of the external world, invoking, for protection, the mighty spirits or gods inhabiting them, was an old ritual according to the Vedic tradition. The Buddha, who disapproves and condemns such superstitious, old practices, gives them new meanings and interpretations, according to the persons to whom he speaks. Cf. 'The Parable of the Piece of Cloth' where he speaks to a brahmin of the 'inner bath' instead of 'sacred baths in holy rivers'. (p. 108.)

holding it sacred, rise early and, leaving Rājagaha, worship in this way.'

'But in the Discipline of the Ārya (Noble One), young house-holder, the six quarters should not be worshipped in this way.'

'How then, sir, in the Discipline of the Ārya, should the six quarters be worshipped? It would be an excellent thing, if the Blessed One would so teach me the way in which according to the Discipline of the Ārya, the six quarters should be worshipped.'

'Hear then, young householder, reflect carefully and I will tell you.'

'Yes, sir,' responded young Sigāla. And the Blessed One said:

'Just as, young householder, the Āryan disciple has put away the four vices in conduct; just as he does no evil actions from the four motives; just as he does not make towards the six doors of dissipating wealth; avoiding these fourteen evil things, he is a guardian of the six quarters, is on his way to conquer both worlds, is successful both in this world and in the next. At the dissolution of the body, after death, he is reborn to a happy destiny in heaven.

'What are the four vices of conduct that he has put away? The destruction of life, stealing, adultery, and lying. These are the four vices of conduct that he has put away.

. . . .

'By which four motives does he do no evil actions? Evil actions are done from motives of partiality, enmity, stupidity and fear. But as the Āryan disciple is not led away by these motives he does no evil actions through them.

. . . .

'And which are the six doors of dissipating wealth? Drink; frequenting the streets at unseemly hours; haunting fairs; gambling; associating with evil friends; idleness.

'There are, young householder, these six dangers of drink: the actual loss of wealth; increase of quarrels; susceptibility to disease; an evil reputation; indecent exposure; ruining one's intelligence.

'Six, young householder, are the perils a man runs through frequenting the streets at unseemly hours: he himself is unguarded or unprotected and so too are his wife and children; so also is his property (wealth); in addition he falls under the suspicion of being responsible for undetected crimes; false rumours are attached to his name; he goes out to meet many troubles.

'There are six perils in haunting fairs: A man keeps looking about to see where is there dancing? where is there singing? music? recitation? cymbal playing? the beating of tam-tams?

'Six, young householder, are the perils of gambling: if the man wins, he is hated; if he loses, he mourns his lost wealth; waste of wealth; his word has no weight in an assembly (a court of law); he is despised by his friends and companions; he is not sought in marriage, for people will say that a man who is a gambler will never make a good husband.

'There are six perils of associating with evil friends: any gambler, any libertine, any tippler, any cheat, any swindler, any man of violence becomes his friend and companion.

'There are six perils in idleness: A man says, it is too cold, and does no work. He says, it is too hot, and does no work; he says, it is too early . . . too late, and does no work. He says, I am too hungry, and does no work . . . too full, and does no work. And while all that he should do remains undone, he makes no money, and such wealth as he has dwindles away.

. . . . .

'Four persons should be reckoned as foes in the likeness of friends: the rapacious person; the man who pays lip-service only to a friend; the flatterer; the wastrel.

'Of these the first is to be reckoned as a foe in the likeness of a friend on four grounds: he is rapacious; he gives little and expects much; he does what he has to do out of fear; he pursues his own interests.

'On four grounds the man who pays lip-service only to a friend is to be reckoned as a foe in the likeness of a friend: he makes friendly professions as regards the past; he makes friendly professions as regards the future; the only service he renders is by his empty sayings; when the opportunity for service arises he shows his unreliability.

'On four grounds the flatterer is to be reckoned as a foe in the likeness of a friend: he approves your bad deeds, as well as your good deeds; he praises you to your face, and in your absence he speaks ill of you.

'On four grounds the wastrel is to be reckoned as a foe in the likeness of a friend: he is your companion when you go drinking; when you frequent the streets at untimely hours; when you haunt shows and fairs; when you gamble.

. . . .

'The friends who should be reckoned as good-hearted (friends) are four: the helper; the friend who is constant in happiness and adversity; the friend of good counsel; the sympathetic friend.

'The friend who is a helper is to be reckoned as good-hearted on four grounds: he protects you when you are taken unawares; he protects your property when you are not there to protect it; he is a refuge to you when you are afraid; when you have tasks to perform he provides twice as much help as you may need.

'The friend who is constant in happiness and adversity is to be reckoned as good-hearted on four grounds: he tells you his secrets; he does not betray your secrets; in your troubles he does not forsake you; for your sake he will even lay down his life.

'The friend of good counsel is . . . good-hearted on four grounds: he restrains you from doing wrong; he enjoins you to (do what is) right; from him you learn what you had not learnt before; he shows you the way to heaven.

'The friend who is sympathetic is to be reckoned as good-hearted on four grounds: he does not rejoice over your misfortunes; he rejoices with you in your prosperity; he restrains those who speak ill of you; he commends those who speak well of you.

. . . .

'And how, young householder, does the Āryan disciple protect (guard) the six quarters?[1] The following should be looked upon as the six quarters: parents as the east; teachers as the south; wife and children as the west; friends and companions as the north; servants and employees as the nadir; recluses and brahmins (the *religieux*) as the zenith.

'A child should minister to his parents as the eastern quarter

[1]Now the Buddha explains to Sigāla what the six quarters are and how to 'worship' them according to the 'Discipline of the Ārya (Noble One)' by way of performing one's duties and obligations towards them, instead of performing the ritual worship according to the old Brahmanic tradition. If the 'six quarters' are 'protected' in this way, they are made safe and secure, and no danger would come from there. Brahmins too worshipped the quarters of the external world to prevent any danger coming from the spirits or gods inhabiting them.

in five ways (saying to himself): Once I was supported by them, now I will be their support; I will perform those duties they have to perform; I will maintain the lineage and tradition of my family; I will look after my inheritance; and I will give alms (perform religious rites) on behalf of them (when they are dead).

'Parents thus ministered to by their children as the eastern quarter, show their love for them in five ways: they restrain them from evil; they direct them towards the good; they train them to a profession; they arrange suitable marriages for them; and in due time, they hand over the inheritance to them.

'In this way the eastern quarter is protected and made safe and secure for him.

'A pupil should minister to his teachers as the southern quarter in five ways: by rising (from his seat, to salute them); by waiting upon them; by his eagerness to learn; by personal service; and by respectfully accepting their teaching.

Teachers, thus ministered to as the southern quarter by their pupil, show their love for their pupil in five ways: they train him well; they make him grasp what he has learnt; they instruct him thoroughly in the lore of every art; they introduce him to their friends and companions; they provide for his security everywhere.

'In this way the southern quarter is protected and made safe and secure for him.

'A wife as western quarter should be ministered to by her husband in five ways: by respecting her; by his courtesy; by being faithful to her; by handing over authority to her; by providing her with adornment (jewellery, etc.).

'The wife, ministered to by her husband as the western quarter, loves him in these five ways: by doing her duty well; by hospitality to attendants, etc.; by her fidelity; by looking after his earnings; and by skill and industry in all her business dealings.

. . . . .

'In this way the western quarter is protected and made safe and secure for him.

'In five ways a member of a family should minister to his friends and companions as the northern quarter: by generosity; by courtesy; by benevolence; by equality (treating them as he treats himself); and by being true to his word.

'Thus ministered to as the northern quarter, his friends and companions love him in these five ways: they protect him when he is in need of protection; they look after his property when he is unable to; they become a refuge in danger; they do not forsake him in his troubles; and they respect even others related to him.

. . . . .

'In this way the northern quarter is protected and made safe and secure for him.

'A master ministers to his servants and employees as the nadir in five ways: by assigning them work according to their capacity and strength; by supplying them with food and wages; by tending them in sickness; by sharing with them unusual delicacies; and by giving them leave and gifts at suitable times.

'In these ways ministered to by their master, servants and employees love their master in five ways: they wake up before him; they go to bed after him; they take what is given to them; they do their work well; and they speak well of him and give him a good reputation.

. . . . .

'In this way is the nadir protected and made safe and secure for him.

'A member of a family (a layman) should minister to recluses and brahmins (the *religieux*) as the zenith in five ways: by affectionate acts; by affectionate words; by affectionate thoughts; by keeping open house for them; by supplying them with their wordly needs.

'In this way ministered to as the zenith, recluses and brahmins show their love for the members of the family (laymen) in six ways: they keep them from evil; they exhort them to do good; they love them with kindly thoughts; they teach them what they have not learnt; they correct and refine what they have learnt; they reveal to them the way to heaven.

'In this way is the zenith protected and made safe and secure for him.'

. . . . .

When the Blessed One had thus spoken, Sigāla the young householder said this: 'Excellent, Sir, excellent! It is as if one should set upright what had been turned upside down, or reveal what had been hidden away, or show the way to a man gone astray, or bring a lamp into darkness so that those with eyes

124

might see things there. In this manner the Dhamma is expounded by the Blessed One in many ways. And I take refuge in the Blessed One, in the Dhamma and in the Community of Bhikkhus. May the Blessed One receive me as his lay-disciple, as one who has taken his refuge in him from this day forth as long as life endures.'

(Digha-Nikāya, No. 31)

THE WORDS OF TRUTH
Selections from
THE *DHAMMAPADA*

1
All (mental) states have mind as their forerunner, mind is their chief, and they are mind-made. If one speaks or acts, with a defiled mind, then suffering follows one even as the wheel follows the hoof of the draught-ox.

2
All (mental) states have mind as their forerunner, mind is their chief, and they are mind-made. If one speaks or acts, with a pure mind, happiness follows one as one's shadow that does not leave one.

3
'He abused me, he beat me, he defeated me, he robbed me': the hatred of those who harbour such thoughts is not appeased.

5
Hatred is never appeased by hatred in this world; it is appeased by love. This is an eternal Law.

24
Whosoever is energetic, mindful, pure in conduct, discriminating, self-restrained, right-living, vigilant, his fame steadily increases.

25

By endeavour, diligence, discipline, and self-mastery, let the wise man make (of himself) an island that no flood can overwhelm.

26

Fools, men of little intelligence, give themselves over to negligence, but the wise man protects his diligence as a supreme treasure.

27

Give not yourselves unto negligence; have no intimacy with sense pleasures. The man who meditates with diligence attains much happiness.

33

This fickle, unsteady mind, difficult to guard, difficult to control, the wise man makes straight, as the fletcher the arrow.

35

Hard to restrain, unstable is this mind; it flits wherever it lists. Good it is to control the mind. A controlled mind brings happiness.

38

He whose mind is unsteady, he who knows not the Good Teaching, he whose confidence wavers, the wisdom of such a person does not attain fullness.

42

Whatever harm a foe may do to a foe, or a hater to another hater, a wrongly-directed mind may do one harm far exceeding these.

43

Neither mother, nor father, nor any other relative can do a man such good as is wrought by a rightly-directed mind.

47

The man who gathers only the flowers (of sense pleasures),

whose mind is entangled, death carries him away as a great flood a sleeping village.

50

One should not pry into the faults of others, into things done and left undone by others. One should rather consider what by oneself is done and left undone.

51

As a beautiful flower that is full of hue but lacks fragrance, even so fruitless is the well-spoken word of one who does not practise it.

61

If, as one fares, one does not find a companion who is better or equal, let one resolutely pursue the solitary course; there can be no fellowship with the fool.

62

'I have sons, I have wealth': thinking thus the fool is troubled. Indeed, he himself is not his own. How can sons or wealth be his?

64

Even if all his life a fool associates with a wise man, he will not understand the Truth, even as the spoon (does not understand) the flavour of the soup.

67

That deed is not well done, which one regrets when it is done and the result of which one experiences weeping with a tearful face.

69

The fool thinks an evil deed as sweet as honey, so long as it does not ripen (does not produce results). But when it ripens, the fool comes to grief.

81

Even as a solid rock is unshaken by the wind, so are the wise unshaken by praise or blame.

82

Even as a lake, deep, extremely clear and tranquil, so do the wise become tranquil having heard the Teaching.

85

Few among men are they who cross to the further shore. The others merely run up and down the bank on this side.

90

For him, who has completed the journey, who is sorrowless, wholly set free, and rid of all bonds, for such a one there is no burning (of the passions).

94

He whose senses are mastered like horses well under the charioteer's control, he who is purged of pride, free from passions, such a steadfast one even the gods envy (hold dear).

96

Calm is the thought, calm the word and deed of him who, rightly knowing, is wholly freed, perfectly peaceful and equipoised.

97

The man who is not credulous, who knows the 'uncreated', who has severed all ties, who has put an end to the occasion (of good and evil), who has vomited all desires, verily he is supreme among men.

103

One may conquer in battle a thousand times a thousand men, yet he is the best of conquerors who conquers himself.

104-105

Better is it truly to conquer oneself than to conquer others. Neither a god, nor an 'angel'[1], nor Māra, nor Brahmā could turn

---

[1] *Gandhabba*, freely rendered as 'angel', refers to a class of semi-divine beings: heavenly musicians.

into defeat the victory of a person such as this who is self-mastered and ever restrained in conduct.

111
Though one may live a hundred years with no true insight and self-control, yet better, indeed, is a life of one day for a man who meditates in wisdom.

116
Make haste in doing good; restrain your mind from evil. Whosoever is slow in doing good, his mind delights in evil.

119
It is well with the evil-doer until his evil (deed) ripens. But when his evil (deed) bears fruit, he then sees its ill effects.

120
It is ill, perhaps, with the doer of good until his good deed ripens. But when it bears fruit, then he sees the happy results.

121
Do not think lightly of evil, saying: 'It will not come to me'. Even a water-pot is filled by the falling of drops. Likewise the fool, gathering it drop by drop, fills himself with evil.

122
Do not think lightly of good, saying: 'It will not come to me'. Even as a water-pot is filled by the falling of drops, so the wise man, gathering it drop by drop, fills himself with good.

125
Whosoever offends an innocent person, pure and guiltless, his evil comes back on that fool himself like fine dust thrown against the wind.

129
All tremble at weapons; all fear death. Comparing others with oneself, one should not slay, nor cause to slay.

He who, seeking his own happiness, torments with the rod creatures that are desirous of happiness, shall not obtain happiness hereafter.

The man of little learning (ignorant) grows like a bull; his flesh grows, but not his wisdom.

Not having lived the Holy Life, not having obtained wealth in their youth, men pine away like old herons in a lake without fish.

If a man practises himself what he admonishes others to do, he himself, being well-controlled, will have control over others. It is difficult, indeed, to control oneself.

Oneself is one's own protector (refuge); what other protector (refuge) can there be? With oneself fully controlled, one obtains a protection (refuge) which is hard to gain.

By oneself indeed is evil done and by oneself is one defiled. By oneself is evil left undone and by oneself indeed is one purified. Purity and impurity depend on oneself. No one can purify another.

Do not follow mean things. Do not dwell in negligence. Do not embrace false views. So the world (i.e. *Saṃsāra*, the cycle of existence and continuity) is not prolonged.

Come, behold this world, how it resembles an ornamented royal chariot, in which fools flounder, but for the wise there is no attachment to it.

178

Better is the gain of Entering the Stream than sole sovereignty over the earth, than going to heaven, than rule supreme over the entire universe.

183

Not to do any evil, to cultivate good, to purify one's mind, this is the Teaching of the Buddhas.

184

The most excellent ascetic practice is patience and forbearance. 'Nibbāna is supreme', say the Buddhas. He indeed is no recluse who harms another; nor is he an ascetic who hurts others.

185

To speak no ill, to do no harm, to practise restraint according to the fundamental precepts, to be moderate in eating, to live in seclusion, to devote oneself to higher consciousness, this is the Teaching of the Buddhas.

197

Happy indeed we live without hate among the hateful. We live free from hatred amidst hateful men.

201

The conqueror begets enmity; the defeated lie down in distress. The peaceful rest in happiness, giving up both victory and defeat.

204

Health is the best gain; contentment is the best wealth. A trusty friend is the best kinsman; *Nibbāna* is the supreme bliss.

205

Having tasted of the flavour of solitude and tranquillity, one becomes woeless and stainless, drinking the essence of the joy of Truth.

215

From lust arises grief; from lust arises fear. For him who is free from lust there is no grief, much less fear.

222

He who holds back arisen anger as one checks a whirling chariot, him I call a charioteer; other folk only hold the reins.

223

Conquer anger by love, evil by good; conquer the miser with liberality, and the liar with truth.

231

Be on your guard against physical agitation; be controlled in body. Forsaking bodily misconduct, follow right conduct in body.

232

Be on your guard against verbal agitation; be controlled in words. Forsaking wrong speech, follow right ways in words.

233

Be on your guard against mental agitation; be controlled in thoughts. Forsaking evil thoughts, follow right ways in thoughts.

234

The wise are controlled in deed, controlled in words, controlled in thoughts, verily, they are fully controlled.

239

By degrees, little by little, from moment to moment, a wise man removes his own impurities, as a smith removes the dross of silver.

240

As rust, arisen out of iron, eats itself away, even so his own deeds lead the transgressor to the states of woe.

248

Know this, O good man, that evil things are uncontrollable. Let not greed and wickedness drag you to suffering for a long time.

251

There is no fire like lust. There is no grip like hate. There is no net like delusion. There is no river like craving.

252

The fault of others is easily seen; but one's own is hard to see. Like chaff one winnows other's' faults; but one's own one conceals as a crafty fowler disguises himself.

267

He who has transcended both merit (good) and demerit (evil), he who leads a pure life, he who lives with understanding in this world, he, indeed, is called a bhikkhu.

268/269

Not by silence does one become a sage (*muni*) if one be foolish and untaught. But the wise man who, as if holding a pair of scales, takes what is good and leaves out what is evil, is indeed a sage. For that reason he is a sage. He who understands both sides in this world is called a sage.

273

Of paths the Eightfold Path is the best; of truths the Four Words (Noble Truths); Detachment is the best of states and of bipeds the Seeing One (the Man of Vision).

274

This is the only Way. There is no other for the purification of Vision. Follow this Way: this is the bewilderment of Māra (Evil).

275

Following this Way you shall make an end of suffering. This verily is the Way declared by me when I had learnt to remove the arrow (of suffering).

276

You yourselves should make the effort; the Awakened Ones are only teachers. Those who enter this Path and who are meditative, are delivered from the bonds of Māra (Evil).

277

'All conditioned things are impermanent', when one sees this in wisdom, then one becomes dispassionate towards the painful. This is the Path to Purity.

278

'All conditioned things are *dukkha* (Ill)', when one sees this in wisdom, then he becomes dispassionate towards the painful. This is the Path to Purity.

279

'All states (*dhamma*) are without self', when one sees this in wisdom, then he becomes dispassionate towards the painful. This is the Path to Purity.

280

Who strives not when he should strive, who, though young and strong, is given to idleness, who is loose in his purpose and thoughts, and who is lazy—that idler never finds the way to wisdom.

281

Watchful of speech, well restrained in mind, let him do no evil with the body; let him purify these three ways of action, and attain the Path made known by the Sages.

334

The craving of the man addicted to careless living grows like a Māluvā creeper. He jumps hither and thither, like a monkey in the forest looking for fruit.

335

Whosoever in this world is overcome by this wretched clinging thirst, his sorrows grow like Bīraṇa grass after rain.

336

But whosoever in this world overcomes this wretched craving so difficult to overcome, his sorrows fall away from him like water-drops from a lotus (leaf).

338

As a tree cut down sprouts forth again if its roots remain uninjured and strong, even so when the propensity to craving is not destroyed, this suffering arises again and again.

343

Led by craving men run this way and that like an ensnared hare. Therefore let the bhikkhu, who wishes his detachment, discard craving.

348

Free thyself from the past, free thyself from the future, free thyself from the present. Crossing to the farther shore of existence, with mind released everywhere, no more shalt thou come to birth and decay.

360

Good is restraint of the eye. Good is restraint of the ear. Good is restraint of the nose. Good is restraint of the tongue.

361

Good is restraint of the body. Good is restraint of speech. Good is restraint of the mind. Restraint everywhere is good. The bhikkhu restrained in every way is freed from all suffering.

362

He who is controlled in hand, controlled in foot, controlled in speech, and possessing the highest control (of mind), delighted within, composed, solitary and contented, him they call a bhikkhu.

365

One should not despise what one receives, and one should not envy (the gain of) others. The bhikkhu who envies others does not attain concentration.

367

He who has no attachment whatsoever to Name and Form (mind and body), and he who does not grieve over what there is not, he indeed is called a bhikkhu.

368

The bhikkhu, who abides in loving-kindness, who is delighted in the Teaching of the Buddha, attains the State of Calm, the happiness of stilling the conditioned things.

385

He for whom there exists neither this shore nor the other, nor both, he who is undistressed and unbound, him I call a brāhman.

387

The sun glows by day; the moon shines by night; in his armour the warrior glows. In meditation shines the brāhman. But all day and night, shines with radiance the Awakened One.

420

He whose destiny neither the gods nor demigods nor men do know, he who has destroyed defilements and become worthy, him I call a brāhman.

423

He who knows former lives, who sees heaven and hell, who has reached the end of births and attained to super-knowledge, the sage, accomplished with all accomplishments, him I call a brāhman.

THE LAST WORDS OF THE BUDDHA

Then the Blessed One addressed the Venerable Ānanda: 'It may be, Ānanda, that to some of you the thought may come: "Here are (we have) the Words of the Teacher who is gone[1]; our Teacher we have with us no more". But Ānanda, it should not be considered in this light. What I have taught and laid down, Ānanda, as Doctrine (*Dhamma*) and Discipline (*Vinaya*), this will, be your teacher when I am gone.

[1] *atītasatthukaṃ pāvacanaṃ.* Rhys Davids' translation: 'The word of the master is ended', does not convey the sense of the original words.

'Just as, Ānanda, the bhikkhus now address one another with the word "Friend" (Āvuso), they should not do so when I am gone. A senior bhikkhu, Ānanda, may address a junior by his name, his family name or with the word "Friend"; a junior bhikkhu should address a senior as "Sir" (Bhante) or "Venerable" (Āyasmā).

'If the Sangha (the Community, the Order) should wish it, Ānanda, let them, when I am gone, abolish the lesser and minor precepts (rules).

'When I am gone, Ānanda, the highest penalty[1] should be imposed on the Bhikkhu Channa.'

'But, Sir, what is the highest penalty?'

'Let the Bhikkhu Channa say what he likes, Ānanda; the bhikkhus should neither speak to him, nor advise him, nor exhort him.'[2]

Then the Blessed One addressed the bhikkhus: 'It may be, Bhikkhus, that there may be doubt or perplexity in the mind of even one bhikkhu about the Buddha, or the Dhamma, or the Sangha, or the Path, or the Practice. Ask Bhikkhus. Do not reproach yourselves afterwards with the thought: "Our Teacher was face to face with us; we could not ask the Blessed One when we were face to face with him". '

When this was said, the bhikkhus remained silent.

A second time and a third time too the Blessed One addressed the bhikkhus . . . as above.

The bhikkhus remained silent even for the third time.

Then the Blessed One addressed them and said: 'It may be, Bhikkhus, that you put no questions out of reverence for your Teacher. Then, Bhikkhus, let friend speak to friend.'[3]

[1]Literally: 'Divine penalty', Brahma-daṇḍa.

[2]Channa was the close companion and charioteer of Prince Siddhārtha before he became the Buddha. Later he entered the Order of the Sangha, was egoistically proud because of his close association with the Master. He tended to be obstinate and self-willed, lacking in proper esprit de corps and often behaving perversely. After the Parinirvāṇa (death) of the Buddha, when Ānanda visited Channa and pronounced on him this penalty of a complete social boycott, even his proud spirit was tamed, he became humble, his eyes were opened. Later he mended his ways and became an Arahant, and the penalty automatically lapsed.

[3]The idea is that if they did not like to put any question directly to the Buddha out of respect for their Teacher, a bhikkhu should whisper the question to his friend, and then the latter could ask it on his behalf.

Even at this, those bhikkhus remained silent.

Then the Venerable Ānanda said to the Blessed One: 'It is wonderful, Sir. It is marvellous, Sir. I have this faith, Sir, in the community of bhikkhus here, that not even one of them has any doubt or perplexity about the Buddha, or the Dhamma, or the Sangha, or the Path, or the Practice.'

'You speak out of faith, Ānanda. But in this matter, Ānanda, the Tathāgata (i.e. Buddha) knows, and knows for certain, that in this community of bhikkhus there is not even one bhikkhu who has any doubt or perplexity about the Buddha, or the Dhamma, or the Sangha, or the Path, or the Practice. Indeed, Ānanda, even the lowest in spiritual attainments among these five hundred bhikkhus is a Stream-entrant (*Sotāpanna*), not liable to fall (into lower states), is assured, and is bound for Enlightenment.'

Then the Blessed One addressed the bhikkhus, saying: 'Then, Bhikkhus, I address you now: Transient are conditioned things. Try to accomplish your aim with diligence.'

These were the last words of the Tathāgata.

(From the *Mahāparinibbāna-sutta* of the *Dīgha-nikāya*, *Sutta* No. 16)

Abbreviations

A: *Aṅguttara-nikāya*, ed. Devamitta Thera (Colombo, 1929) and PTS edition.

Abhisamuc: *Abhidharma-samuccaya* of Asanga, ed. Pradhan (Visvabharati, Santiniketan, 1950).

D: *Dīgha-nikāya*, ed. Nānāvāsa Thera (Colombo, 1929).

DA: *Dīgha-nikāyaṭṭhakathā, Sumaṅgalavilāsinī* (Simon Hewavitarne Bequest Series, Colombo).

Dhp: *Dhammapada*, ed. K. Dhammaratana Thera (Colombo, 1926).

DhpA: *Dhammapadaṭṭhakathā* (PTS edition).

Dhs: *Dhammasaṅgaṇi,* (PTS ed.)

Laṅkā: *The Laṅkāvatāra-sūtra*, ed. Nanjio (Kyoto, 1923).

M: *Majjhima-nikāya* (PTS edition).

MA: *Majjhima-nikāyaṭṭhakathā, Papañcasūdanī* (PTS edition).

Madhyakāri: *Mādhyamika-Kārikā* of Nāgārjuna, ed. L. de La Vallée Poussin (Bib. Budd. IV).

Mh-Sūtrālankāra: *Mahāyāna-sūtrālaṅkāra* of Asanga, ed. Sylvain Levi (Paris, 1907).

Mhvg: *Mahāvagga (of the Vinaya)*, ed. Saddhātissa Thera (Alutgama, 1922).

PTS: Pali Text Society of London.

Prmj: *Paramatthajotikā* (PTS edition).

S: *Saṃyutta-nikāya* (PTS edition).

Sārattha: *Sāratthappakāsinī* (PTS edition).

Sn: *Suttanipāta* (PTS edition).

Ud: *Udāna* (Colombo, 1929).

Vibh: *Vibhaṅga* (PTS edition).

Vism: *Visuddhimagga* (PTS edition).

Selected Bibliograghy

FOR THE ENGLISH READER

ARNOLD, SIR EDWIN: *The Light of Asia* (in many editions).

BURTT, EDWIN A.: *The Teaching of the Compassionate Buddha* (The New American Library, 1955).

CONZE, HORNER, SNELLGROW, WALEY: *Buddhist Texts Through the Ages* (Bruno Cassirer, Oxford).

DALKE, PAUL: *Buddhism* (Macmillan, London); *Buddhist Essays* (Macmillan, London); *Buddhism and Science* (Macmillan, London).

DHAMMAPALA, BHIKKHU: *Basic Buddhism* (The Associated Newspapers of Ceylon, Ltd., Colombo).

EVOLA, J.: *The Doctrine of Awakening* (Luzac & Co., London).

HUMPHREYS, CHRISTMAS: *Buddhism* (Pelican Series).

LOUNSBERY, G. CONSTANT: *Buddhist Meditation* (Luzac & Co., London).

LUDOWYK, E. F. C.: *The Footprint of the Buddha* (George Allen & Unwin, London, 1958).

MALALASEKERA, G. P.: *The Buddha and His Teachings* (The Lanka Bauddha Mandalaya, Colombo).

NARADA, MAHATHERA: *Buddhism in a Nutshell* (The Associated Newspapers of Ceylon, Colombo).

NYANAPONIKA, THERA: *Manual of Buddhism* (The Associated Newspapers of Ceylon, Colombo); *The Heart of Buddhist Meditation* (Colombo, 1954).

NYANATILOKA, MAHATHERA: *The Essence of Buddhism* (The Associated Newspapers of Ceylon, Colombo); *The Fundamentals of Buddhism* (The Associated Newspapers of Ceylon, Colombo); *The Word of the Buddha* (The Associated Newspapers of Ceylon, Colombo).

RAHULA, WALPOLA: *History of Buddhism in Ceylon* (M. D. Gunasena & Co., Colombo, 1956).

RHYS DAVIDS, T. W.: *Buddhism, American Lectures* (Putnam, London).

SURIYABONGS, DR. LUANG: *Buddhism in the Light of Modern Scientific Ideas* (Bangkok, Thailand).

TACHIBANA, S.: *The Ethics of Buddhism* (The Maha Bodhi Society. Colombo).

THOMAS, E. J.: *Early Buddhist Scriptures* (Kegan Paul, London); *The Life of Buddha as Legend and History* (Kegan Paul, London); *History of Buddhist Thought* (Kegan Paul, London); *The Road to Nirvāṇa* (The Wisdom of the East Series, John Murray, London); *The Quest of Enlightenment* (John Murray, London).

WARREN, HENRY CLARK: *Buddhism in Translation* (Harvard University Press, U.S.A.).

WOODWARD, F. L.: *Some Sayings of the Buddha* (World's Classics, Oxford); *The Buddha's Path of Virtue* (The Translation of the *Dhammapada*) (Adyar, Madras, India).

Glossary

Ācariya, teacher.

Ācariya-muṭṭhi, 'closed fist of the teacher', i.e., esoteric doctrine, secret teaching.

Adhamma, evil, wrong, unjust, immoral.

Adhimokkha, determination.

Ādīnava, evil consequence, danger, unsatisfactoriness.

Āhāra, nutriment.

Ajjava, honesty, integrity.

Akkodha, freedom from hatred.

Akusala, unwholesome, demerit, wrong, bad, evil.

Ālaya-vijñāna, 'store-consciousness'.

Amata (Skt. *Amṛta*), immortality. synonym for Nirvāṇa.

Anāgāmi, 'Non-returner', the third stage in the realization of Nirvāṇa.

Ānāpānasati, mindfulness of in-and-out-breathing, a form of meditation.

Anatta, No-Soul, No-Self.

Anicca, impermanent.

Arahant, one who is free from all fetters, defilements and impurities through the realization of Nirvāṇa in the fourth and final stage, and who is free from rebirth.

Ariya-aṭṭhaṅgika-magga, Noble Eightfold Path.

Ariya-sacca, Noble Truth.

Assāda, enjoyment, attraction.

Atakkāvacara, beyond logic.

Ātman (Pali *Attā*), soul, self, ego.

Attadīpa, holding oneself as one's own island (protection).

Attasaraṇa, holding oneself as one's own refuge.

Avihiṃsā (=*Ahiṃsā*), non-violence.

Avijjā, ignorance, illusion, delusion.

Avirodha, non-obstruction, non-opposition.

Āvuso, friend (form of address among equals).

Avyākata (with regard to problems) unexplained, not declared; (ethically) neutral, (neither good nor bad).

Āyasmā, venerable.

Āyatana, 'Sphere'. Six internal spheres: eye, ear, nose, tongue, body and mind; six external spheres: visible form, sound, odour, taste, tangible things and mind-objects (ideas, thoughts, conceptions).

Bhaiṣajya-guru, Doctor of Medicine.
Bhante, Sir, Venerable Sir.
Bhava, becoming, existence, continuity.
Bhāvanā, 'meditation', mental culture.
Bhikkhu, Buddhist monk, mendicant monk.
Bhisakka, doctor, physician.
Bodhi, Bo-tree, the Tree of Wisdom, *Ficus religiosa*, the tree under which the Buddha attained Enlightenment.
Bojjhaṅga, factors of Enlightenment.
Brahma, supreme being, creator of the universe.
Brāhmaṇa, a Brahmin, member of the highest caste in India.
Brahma-vihāra, supreme dwelling (in universal love, compassion, sympathetic joy and equanimity).
Buddha, Awakened One, Enlightened One.

Cetanā, volition.
Chanda, will.
Citta, mind.
Cittekaggatā, one-pointedness of mind.

Dāgäba, Sinhalese word derived from Pali *Dhātu-gabbha* or Skt. *Dhātu-garbha* which means lit. 'relic-chamber'; a dome-like solid structure in which the relics of the Buddha are enshrined; a *stūpa*.
Dāna, charity.
Dasa-rāja-dhamma, the Ten Duties of the King.
Deva, a deity, a celestial being, a god.
Dhamma (Skt. *Dharma*), Truth, Teaching, doctrine, righteousness, piety, morality, justice, nature, all things and states conditioned or unconditioned, etc.
Dhamma-cakka, wheel of Truth.
Dhamma-cakkhu, 'Eye of Truth'.
Dhamma-vicaya, search of Truth.
Dhamma-vijaya, conquest by piety.
Dhyāna, 'trance', *recueillement*, a state of mind achieved through higher meditation.
Dosa, anger, hatred, ill-will.
Dravya, substance.
Dukkha, suffering, conflict, unsatisfactoriness, unsubstantiality, emptiness.

Ehi-passika, lit. 'Come and see', a phrase used to describe the teaching of the Buddha.

Hinayāna, 'Small Vehicle', a term coined and used by the Mahāyānists referring to earlier orthodox sects (or schools) of Buddhism. See *Mahāyāna* and *Theravāda*.

Indriya, faculty, a sense-faculty, a sense-organ.

Jāti, birth.
Jarā-maraṇa, old age and death.

Kabaliṅkārāhāra, material food.
Kalyāṇa-mitta, a good friend, who leads you along the right path.
Kāma, sense-pleasures, desire for sense-pleasures.
Kamma (Skt. *Karma*), volitional action, lit. action, deed.
Kamma-phala, *Kamma-vipāka*, the fruit or result of action.
Karuṇā, compassion.
Khandha, aggregate.
Khanti, patience, forbearance, tolerance.
Kilesa, defilements, impurities, passions.
Kṣatriya, royal caste, the second caste in the Indian caste system, a member of that caste.
Kusala, wholesome, merit, good.

Maddava, gentleness, softness.
Magga, Path, Way.
Mahā-bhūta, great elements. (Four in number: solidity, fluidity, heat and motion).
Mahāyāna, 'Great Vehicle', form of Buddhism of later development, now mainly followed in China, Japan, Korea and Tibet. See *Hīnayāna* and *Theravāda*.
Majjhimā-paṭipadā, Middle Path.
Māna, pride.
Manas, mental organ, mind.
Manasikāra, attention.
Manosañcetanāhāra, mental volition as nutriment.
Mettā, love, universal love, lit. 'friendship'.
Micchā-diṭṭhi, wrong view, wrong opinion.
Moha, ignorance, delusion, illusion.
Muditā, sympathetic joy, joy for others' success, welfare and happiness.

Nairātmya, soullessness, the fact that there is no Self.
Nāma-rūpa, Name and Form, mental and physical energies.
Ñāṇa-dassana, insight, vision through wisdom.
Nirodha, cessation.
Nirvāṇa, Pāli *Nibbāna*, the Buddhist *summum bonum*, Ultimate Reality,
Absolute Truth, lit. 'blowing out, extinction'.
Nissaraṇa, freedom, liberation, lit. 'going out'.
Nīvaraṇa, hindrance, obstruction.

Pañcakkhandha, Five Aggregates (matter, sensation, perception, mental
activities and consciousness).
Paññā, wisdom.
Paramattha (Skt. *Paramārtha*), Absolute Truth, Ultimate Reality.
Pariccāga, giving up, renouncing.
Parinirvāṇa (Pali *Parinibbāna*), 'fully blowing out', the final passing away
of the Buddha or an Arahant.
Passaddhi, relaxation.
Paṭicca-samuppāda, Conditioned Genesis, (Dependent Origination).
Paṭigha, repugnance, anger.
Paṭisotagāmi, going against the current.
Paṭivedha, penetration, deep understanding.
Phassa, contact.
Phassāhāra, contact as nutriment, (contact of internal sense-faculties
with the external world as nutriment).
Pīti, joy.
Puggala, Skt. *Pudgala*, individual, person.

Rāga, lust, desire.
Ratanattaya, Triple-Gem: the Buddha, the Dhamma (his Teaching)
and the Sangha (the Order of Monks).
Rūpa, matter, form.

Sacca (Skt. *Satya*), Truth.
Saddhā, Skt. *Śraddhā*, confidence (faith, belief).
Sakadāgāmi, 'Once-Returner', the second stage in the realization of
Nirvāṇa.
Sakkāya-diṭṭhi, belief in a Soul or Self.
Saḷāyatana, six spheres. See *Āyatana*.

Samādhi, concentration attained through higher meditation, mental discipline.

Samajīvikatā, living within one's means.

Samatha, tranquillity, concentration.

Saṃkhāra, saṃkhata, conditioned things and states.

Sammā-ājīva, right livelihood.

Sammā-diṭṭhi, right view.

Sammā-kammanta, right action.

Sammā-samādhi, right concentration.

Sammā-saṃkappa, right thought.

Sammā-sati, right mindfulness.

Sammā-vācā, right speech.

Sammā-vāyāma, right effort.

Sammuti, convention, *sammuti-sacca*, conventional truth.

Saṃsāra, continuity of existence, cycle of existence.

Samudaya, arising, origin of *dukkha*, the Second Noble Truth.

Saṅgha, Community of Buddhist monks.

Saññā, perception.

Sassata-vāda, eternalism, eternalistic theory.

Sati, mindfulness, awareness.

Satipaṭṭhāna, setting-up of mindfulness.

Satthā, teacher, master.

Sīla, virtue, morality.

Sotāpanna, 'Stream-entrant', the first stage in the realization of Nirvāṇa.

Stūpa, see *Dāgäba*.

Śūdra, low caste, the fourth caste in the Indian caste system, a member of this caste.

Sukha, happiness, ease, comfort.

Sutta, discourse, sermon.

Taṇhā (Skt. *Tṛṣṇā*), 'thirst', desire, craving.

Taṇhakkhaya, 'extinction of thirst', synonym for Nirvāṇa.

Tapa, austerity.

Tathāgata, 'One who has found the Truth', synonym for Buddha, a term generally used by the Buddha referring to himself or to other Buddhas. *Tatha* (truth) plus *āgata* (come, arrived).

Thera-vāda, 'The system or School of the Elders', considered to be the orthodox and original form of Buddhism as accepted and followed mainly in Ceylon, Burma, Thailand, Laos and Chittagong. See *Mahāyāna* and *Hīnayāna*.

Thīna-middha, torpor and languor.

Tipiṭaka, Skt. *Tripiṭaka*, Three Books, usually called 'Three Baskets'. The three main canonical divisions of the Buddha's teaching into *Vinaya* (Code of Discipline), *Sutta* (Discourses) and *Abhidhamma* (Higher Doctrine, Philosophy and Psychology).

Tisaraṇa, Three Refuges: The Buddha, the Dhamma (Teaching) and the Sangha (the Community of Monks).

Uccheda-vāda, annihilationism, annihilationist theory.

Uddhacca-kukkucca, restlessness and worry, 'flurry and worry'.

Upādāna, grasping, attachment.

Upādāyarūpa, derivative matter.

Upāsaka, a lay Buddhist.

Upekkhā, equanimity.

Vaiśya, agricultural and trader caste, third caste in the Indian caste system, a member of this caste.

Vedanā, sensation, feeling.

Vibhava, annihilation, *vibhava-taṇhā*, desire for annihilation.

Vicikicchā, doubt.

Viññāṇa, consciousness.

Viññāṇāhāra, consciousness as nutriment.

Vipāka, result, consequence.

Vipariṇāma, change, transformation, alteration.

Vipassanā, insight, analytical insight.

Virāga, detachment, freedom from desire.

Viriya, energy.

Vyāpāda, anger, hatred, ill-will.

Yathā-bhūta, in reality, as things are.

Index

Printed at Haw Chai Printing Co., Ltd.